# THE
# WRITER
# AND THE
# READER

# THE WRITER AND THE READER

## A BOOK OF
## LITERARY QUOTATIONS

*Neil Ewart*

BLANDFORD PRESS
POOLE · DORSET

*First published*
*in the UK 1984*
*by Blandford Press*
*Link House*
*West Street, Poole, Dorset, BH15 1LL*

*Compilation copyright © 1984*
*Neil Ewart*

*Distributed in*
*the United States by*
*Sterling Publishing Co., Inc.,*
*2 Park Avenue, New York,*
*N.Y. 10016, USA*

**British Library Cataloguing in Publication Data**

Ewart, Neil
  The writer and the reader.
  1. Quotations, English
  I. Title
  082          PN6081

*ISBN 0 7137 1403 4*

*Typeset by August Filmsetting, Haydock, St Helens*
*in 10/12 pt Monophoto Ehrhardt*

*Printed and bound in Great Britain by*
*Biddles Ltd, Guildford and King's Lynn*

# Contents

# Introduction

Although writing isn't easy, it is certainly one of the most enjoyable and satisfying of all occupations, or hobbies. History shows that it is possible for people from all walks of life to succeed as writers, provided they are determined to do so. For, as Pubilius Syrus observed in the first century BC, 'No one knows what they can do until they try'.

Age has nothing to do with success – fortunes have been made (and still are being made) by authors and writers aged 50 or over, as well as by younger ones. Almost all the great poetry of past centuries was written by poets who were under 25, and much of the rest by those under 30. Success is seldom instant, however. Jane Austen found it difficult to get her works published at first, and so did William Makepeace Thackeray when he wrote *Vanity Fair*. Hans Christian Andersen's *Fairy Tales* were turned down by publisher after publisher. The examples are endless.

In more recent times Susan Howatch received repeated rejections of her novel *Penmarric* from English publishers, until she offered it in America, where it not only became an immediate bestseller but, subsequently, sold by the million in the UK. Her second novel *Cashelmara* made even more money than her previous massive saga. James Herriot's original stories about his experience as a veterinary surgeon were turned down time and again before they found a receptive publisher. The rest is publishing history; his books have sold millions; and he did not start writing until he was 50.

It is not only novels and children's books that make fortunes, but textbooks and other non-fiction books. Ronald Ridout is one outstanding example as his numerous textbooks have sold tens of millions of copies.

The quotations and observations included in this book have been selected not only to offer valuable advice from the personal experiences of the greatest writers of 2,500 years but also to provide interesting and entertaining reading for reader and writer, or would-be writer, alike. The arrangement is such that quotations giving one point of view are frequently followed by those expressing opposing ones, and others are included every now and again to provide light relief, or to make the book more informative, thought-provoking, and enjoyable.

Some of the quotations appear modern but, in fact, come to us from many centuries ago. An Index of Authors has been included, therefore, so that each can be placed in time.

If your interest is in reading what others have written, you may find yourself agreeing with many of the thoughts expressed throughout this book, including Ralph Waldo Emerson's observation that: 'In the highest civilization the book is still the highest delight.' If you are an established writer you will, no doubt, side with Oliver Wendell Holmes' view of critics: 'What a blessed thing it is that Nature, when she invented, manufactured and patented her authors, contrived to make critics out of the chips that were left!' You may also feel sympathy for James Huneker who regarded critics as 'men who expect miracles'.

If you are new to the craft of writing, persevere, and refuse to be put off, and then you may succeed. You will most certainly find with Walter Bagehot that: 'The great pleasure in life is doing what people say you cannot do.'

# 1
# Books

*Blest be the hour wherein I bought this book;*
*His studies happy that composed the book,*
*And the man fortunate that sold the book.*
        BEN JONSON, *Every Man in his Humour*

*I love my books as drinkers love their wine;*
*The more I drink, the more they seem divine.*
        FRANCIS BENNOCH, *My Books*

Books are the most mannerly of companions, accesible at all times, in all moods, frankly declaring the author's mind, without offence.
        AMOS BRONSON ALCOTT, *Concord Days*

Let your bookcases and your shelves be your gardens and your pleasure-grounds. Pluck the fruit that grows therein, gather the roses, the spices, and the myrrh.
        IBN TIBBON, *Abrahams, Jewish Life in the Middle Ages*

*Dreams, books, are each a world; and books, we know,*
*Are a substantial world, both pure and good:*
*Round these, with tendrils strong as flesh and blood,*
*Our pastime and our happiness will grow.*
        WILLIAM WORDSWORTH, *Personal Talk*

Books are the compasses and telescopes and sextants and charts which other men have prepared to help us navigate the dangerous seas of human life.
        JESSE LEE BENNETT, *Books as Guides*

Books are the blessed chloroform of the mind.
>ROBERT CHAMBERS, *What English Literature Gives Us*

Of the things which man can do or make here below, by far the most momentous, wonderful, and worthy are the things we call Books!
>THOMAS CARLYLE, *On Heroes and Hero-Worship*,
>'The Hero as Man of Letters'

A book is a friend whose face is constantly changing. If you read it when you are recovering from an illness, and return to it years after, it is changed surely, with the change in yourself.
>ANDREW LANG, *The Library*

All books are divisible into two classes: the books of the hour, and the books of all time.
>JOHN RUSKIN, *Sesame and Lilies*

I love to lose myself in other men's minds. When I am not walking, I am reading; I cannot sit and think. Books think for me.
>CHARLES LAMB, *Last Essays of Elia*, 'Detached Thoughts
>on Books and Reading'

The true University of these days is a collection of books.
>THOMAS CARLYLE, *On Heroes and Hero-Worship*,
>'The Hero as Man of Letters'

Some books are read in the parlour and some in the kitchen, but the test of a real genuine book is that it is read in both.
>THOMAS CHANDLER HALIBURTON, *Wise Saws*

The best companions are the best books.
>LORD CHESTERFIELD, *Letter to Lord Huntingdon*, c.1760

I cannot live without books.
>THOMAS JEFFERSON, *Letter to John Adams*, 1815

My books are friends that never fail me.
>THOMAS CARLYLE, *Letter to his Mother*, 1817

The reading of all good books is like a conversation with the finest men of past centuries.

RENÉ DESCARTES, *Le Discours de la Méthode*

Wear the old coat and buy the new book.

AUSTIN PHELPS, *Theory of Preaching*

In the highest civilization the book is still the highest delight.

RALPH WALDO EMERSON, *Letters and Social Aims*,
'Quotation and Originality'

Books are a guide in youth, and an entertainment for age. They support us under solitude, and keep us from becoming a burden to ourselves. They help us forget the crossness of men and things, compose our cares and our passions, and lay our disappointments asleep. When we are weary of the living, we may repair to the dead, who have nothing of peevishness, pride or design in their conversation.

JEREMY COLLIER, *Of the Entertainment of Books*

Books are the legacies that a great genius leaves to mankind, which are delivered down from generation to generation, as presents to the posterity of those who are yet unborn.

JOSEPH ADDISON, *The Spectator*, 10 Sept, 1711

Books, like proverbs, receive their chief value from the stamp and esteem of ages through which they have passed.

SIR WILLIAM TEMPLE, *Miscellanea*, 'Ancient
and Modern Learning'

> *Give a man a book he can read;*
> *And his home is bright with a calm delight,*
> *Though the room be poor indeed.*

JAMES THOMSON, *Gifts*

It is chiefly through books that we enjoy intercourse with superior minds . . . In the best books, great men talk to us, give us their most precious thoughts, and pour their souls into ours. God be thanked for books. They are the voices of the distant and the dead, and make us heirs of the spiritual life of past ages. Books are true levellers. They give to all, who will faithfully use them, the society, the spiritual presence, of the best and greatest of our race.

WILLIAM ELLERY CHANNING, *Self-Culture*

All that mankind has done, thought, gained or been: it is lying as in magic preservation in the pages of books.

THOMAS CARLYLE, *On Heroes and Hero-Worship*,
'The Hero as Man of Letters'

'Tis the good reader that makes the good book; in every book he finds passages which seem confidences or asides hidden from all else and unmistakably meant for his ear; the profit of books is according to the sensibility of the reader; the profoundest thought or passion sleeps as in a mine, until it is discovered by an equal mind and heart.

RALPH WALDO EMERSON, *Society and Solitude*,
'Success'

Many books require no thought from those who read them, for a very simple reason – they made no such demand upon those who wrote them. Those works, therefore, are the most valuable that set our thinking faculties in the fullest operation.

CHARLES CALEB COLTON, *Lacon*

The books which help you most are those which make you think the most.

THEODORE PARKER, *World of Matter and World of Men*

Books must be read as deliberately and reservedly as they were written.

HENRY DAVID THOREAU, *Walden*, 'Reading'

We find little in a book but what we put there. But in great books, the mind finds room to put many things.

JOSEPH JOUBERT, *Pensées*

The very cheapness of literature is making even wise people forget that if a book is worth reading, it is worth buying. No book is worth anything which is not worth much; nor is it serviceable, until it has been read, and re-read, and loved, and loved again; and marked, so that you can refer to the passages you want in it.

JOHN RUSKIN, *Sesame and Lilies*

Classics which at home are drowsily read have a strange charm in a country inn, or in the transom of a merchant brig.

RALPH WALDO EMERSON, *English Traits*

*For some in ancient books delight;*
*Others prefer what moderns write:*
*Now I should be extremely loth*
*Not to be thought expert in both.*

MATTHEW PRIOR, *Alma*

He (Pliny the Elder) used to say that 'no book was so bad but some good might be got out of it'.

PLINY THE YOUNGER, *Letters*

Some books are to be tasted, others to be swallowed, and some few to be chewed and digested.

FRANCIS BACON, *Essays*, 'Of Studies'

Of all the needs a book has the chief need is that it be readable.

ANTHONY TROLLOPE, *Autobiography*

I have somewhere seen it observed, that we should make the same use of a book that the bee does of a flower: she steals sweets from it, but does not injure it.

CHARLES CALEB COLTON, *Lacon*

When I take up a work that I have read before (the oftener the better) I know what I have to expect. The satisfaction is not lessened by being anticipated.

WILLIAM HAZLITT, *The Plain Speaker*,
'On Reading Old Books'

A man who attempts to read all the new productions must do as the fleas do – skip.

SAMUEL ROGERS, Attributed

I love everything that's old; old friends, old times, old manners, old books, old wines.

OLIVER GOLDSMITH, *She Stoops to Conquer*

Some will read old books, as if there were no valuable truths to be discovered in modern publications.

ISAAC D'ISRAELI, *Literary Miscellanies*

*Books give not wisdom where was none before,*
*But where some is, there reading makes it more.*
SIR JOHN HARINGTON, *Epigrams*

Of all the inanimate objects, of all men's creations, books are the nearest to us, for they contain our very thoughts, our ambitions, our indignations, our illusions, our fidelity to truth, and our persistent leaning toward error. But most of all they resemble us in their precarious hold on life.

JOSEPH CONRAD, *Notes on Life and Letters*

*The love of learning, the sequestered nooks,*
*And all the sweet serenity of books.*
HENRY WADSWORTH LONGFELLOW, *Morituri Salutamus*

Buy good books and read them; the best books are the commonest, and the last editions are always the best, if the editors are not blockheads, for they may profit of the former.

LORD CHESTERFIELD, *Letters*, 1750

Books are the quietest and most constant of friends; they are the most accessible and wisest of counsellors, and the most patient of teachers.

CHARLES WILLIAM ELIOT, *The Happy Life*

The only important thing in a book is the meaning it has for you.
SOMERSET MAUGHAM, *The Summing Up*

It is saying less than the truth to affirm that an excellent book (and the remark holds almost equally good of a Raphael as of a Milton) is like a well-chosen and well-tended fruit tree. Its fruits are not of one season only. With the due and natural intervals, we may recur to it year after year, and it will supply the same nourishment and the same gratification, if only we ourselves return to it with the same healthful appetite.
SAMUEL TAYLOR COLERIDGE, *Prospectus of Lectures*

Books take their place according to their specific gravity as surely as potatoes in a tub.
RALPH WALDO EMERSON, *Journals*, 1834

No good Book, or good thing of any sort, shows its best face at first.
THOMAS CARLYLE, *Essays*, 'Novalis'

The easiest books are generally the best; for, whatever author is obscure and difficult in his own language, certainly does not think clearly.
LORD CHESTERFIELD, *Letter to his son*, 1750

Most of today's books have an air of having been written in one day from books read the night before.
SÉBASTIEN ROCH NICOLAS CHAMFORT, *Maximes et pensées*

There are books of which the backs and covers are by far the best parts.
CHARLES DICKENS, *Oliver Twist*

Many thanks; I shall lose no time in reading it.
BENJAMIN DISRAELI, Reply on receiving unsolicited manuscript from author

There is as much trickery required to grow rich by a stupid book as there is folly in buying it.

JEAN DE LA BRUYÈRE, *Les Caractères*

*Books cannot always please, however good;*
*Minds are not ever craving for their food.*

GEORGE CRABBE, *The Borough*

What a convenient and delightful world is this world of books! – if you bring to it not the obligations of the student, or look upon it as an opiate for idleness, but enter it rather with the enthusiasm of the adventurer!

DAVID GRAYSON, *Adventures in Contentment*

In books lies the sound of the whole past time.

THOMAS CARLYLE, *On Heroes and Hero-Worship*,
'The Heroic in History'

A room without books is as a body without a soul.

MARCUS TULLIUS CICERO, *Lubbock, Pleasures of Life*

A book is good company. It is full of conversation without loquacity. It comes to your longing with full instruction, but pursues you never.

HENRY WARD BEECHER, *Proverbs from Plymouth Pulpit*

The test of a first-rate work, and a test of your sincerity in calling it a first-rate work, is that you finish it.

ARNOLD BENNETT, *Things that have Interested Me*

A book is made better by good readers and clearer by good opponents.

FRIEDRICH NIETZSCHE, *Miscellaneous Maxims and Opinions*

*Books are a part of man's prerogative;*
*In formal ink they thoughts and voices hold,*
*That we to them our solitude may give,*
*And make time present travel that of old.*

SIR THOMAS OVERBURY, *A Wife*

Man builds no structure which outlives a book.

> EUGENE FITCH WARE, *The Book*

One would imagine that books were, like women, the worse for being old; that they have a pleasure in being read for the first time; that they open their leaves more cordially; that the spirit of enjoyment wears out with the spirit of novelty; and that, after a certain age, it is high time to put them on the shelf.

> WILLIAM HAZLITT, *Essays*, 'On Reading New Books'

When a new book is published, read an old one.

> SAMUEL ROGERS, Attributed

That is a good book which is opened with expectation and closed with profit.

> AMOS BRONSON ALCOTT, *Table Talk*, 'Learning-Books'

Lo, here a little volume, but a great book!

> RICHARD CRASHAW, *Preface to a little Prayer-Book*

A good book is the precious life-blood of a master spirit, embalmed and treasured up on purpose to a life beyond life.

> JOHN MILTON, *Areopagitica*

A good book is the purest essence of a human soul.

> THOMAS CARLYLE, Speech in support of the London Library, 1840

A good book is the best of friends, the same today and for ever.

> MARTIN FARQUHAR TUPPER, *Proverbial Philosophy*, 'Of Reading'

All the world may know me by my book, and my book by me.

> MICHEL DE MONTAIGNE, *Essays*, Bk. 3

A wise man will select his books, for he would not wish to class them all under the sacred name of friends. Some can be accepted only as acquaintances. The best books of all kinds are taken to the heart, and cherished as his most precious possessions. Others to be chatted with for a time, to spend a few pleasant hours with, and laid aside, but not forgotten.

JOHN ALFRED LANGFORD, *The Praise of Books*, Preliminary Essay

A man is known by the company his mind keeps.

THOMAS BAILEY ALDRICH, *Leaves from a Notebook*,
'Ponkapog Papers'

A book may be amusing with numerous errors, or it may be very dull without a single absurdity.

OLIVER GOLDSMITH, *The Vicar of Wakefield*, Preface

I cannot see that lectures can do so much good as reading the books from which the lectures are taken.

SAMUEL JOHNSON, Quoted in Boswell's *Life of Johnson*

What can we see, read, acquire, but ourselves. Take the book, my friend, and read your eyes out, you will never find there what I find.

RALPH WALDO EMERSON, *Journals*, 1832

*Books should to one of these four ends conduce,*
*For wisdom, piety, delight, or use.*

SIR JOHN DENHAM, *Of Prudence*

If a book come from the heart, it will contrive to reach other hearts; all art and authorcraft are of small amount to that.

THOMAS CARLYLE, *On Heroes and Hero-Worship*,
'The Hero as Man of Letters'

Books are the treasured wealth of the world, the fit inheritance of generations and nations.

HENRY DAVID THOREAU, *Walden*, 'Reading'

When I get hold of a book I particularly admire, I am so enthusiastic that I loan it to some one who never brings it back.

EDGAR WATSON HOWE, *Country Town Sayings*

Please return this book; I find that though many of my friends are poor arithmeticians, they are nearly all good book-keepers.

SIR WALTER SCOTT, Inscription in one of his Books

Never lend books, for no one ever returns them; the only books I have in my library are books that other folk have lent me.

ANATOLE FRANCE, *La Vie Littéraire*

I take the view, and always have done, that if you cannot say what you have to say in twenty minutes, you should go away and write a book about it.

LORD BRABAZON, Quoted in a Press report, 1955

Edward Fitzgerald said that he wished we had more lives of obscure persons; one wants to know what other people are thinking and feeling about it all . . . If the dullest person in the world would only put down sincerely what he or she thought about his or her life, about work and love, religion and emotion, it would be a fascinating document.

ARTHUR CHRISTOPHER BENSON, *From a College Window*

*When I am dead, I hope it may be said:*
*'His sins were scarlet, but his books were read'.*

HILAIRE BELLOC, *On His Books*

The globe we inhabit is divided into two worlds: the common geographical world, and the world of books; . . . in habit and perception between real and unreal, we may say that we more frequently wake out of common life to them, than out of them to common life.

JAMES HENRY LEIGH HUNT, *Monthly Repository*,
Farewell Address, 1828

We are too civil to books. For a few golden sentences we will turn over and actually read a volume of four or five hundred pages.

RALPH WALDO EMERSON, *Journals*, 1841

*Whence is thy learning? Hath thy toil*
*O'er books consum'd the midnight oil?*

JOHN GAY, *Fables*

The foolishest book is a kind of leaky boat on a sea of wisdom; some of the wisdom will get in somehow.

OLIVER WENDELL HOLMES, *Poet at the Breakfast Table*

A bad book is generally a very easy book, having been composed by its author with no labour of mind whatever; whereas a good book, though it be not necessarily a hard one, yet, since it contains important facts, duly arranged, and reasoned upon with care, must require from the reader some portion of the same attention and study to comprehend and profit by it, as it required from the writer to compose it.

PETER MERE LATHAM, *Collected Works*

To sit alone in the lamplight with a book spread out before you, and hold intimate converse with men of unseen generations – such is a pleasure beyond compare.

YOSHIDA KENKŌ, *Tsurezure-Gusa*, 'Essays in Idleness'

*I shall be found by the fire, suppose,*
*O'er a great wise book as beseemeth age,*
*While the shutters flap as the cross-wind blows*
*And I turn the page, and I turn the page,*
*Not verse now, only prose!*

ROBERT BROWNING, *By the Fireside*

How many a man has dated a new era in his life from the reading of a book.

HENRY DAVID THOREAU, *Walden*, 'Reading'

The most accomplished way of using books at present is two-fold: either, first, to serve them as some men do lords, learn their titles exactly, and then brag of their acquaintance. Or, secondly, which is indeed the choicer, the profounder, and politer method, to get a thorough insight into the index, by which the whole book is governed and turned, like fishes by the tail.

JONATHAN SWIFT, *A Tale of a Tub*

He (Shakespeare) was naturally learned; he needed not the spectacles of books to read nature; he looked inwards, and found her there.

JOHN DRYDEN, *Essay of Dramatic Poesy*

> The Love of Books, the Golden Key
> That opens the Enchanted Door.
>
> ANDREW LANG, *Ballade of the Bookworm*

In old days books were written by men of letters and read by the public. Nowadays books are written by the public and read by nobody.

OSCAR WILDE, *Saturday Review*, 1894

It is with books as with men – a very small number play a great part; the rest are lost in the multitude.

VOLTAIRE, *Books – Philosophical Dictionary*

Books have always a secret influence on the understanding; we cannot at pleasure obliterate ideas: he that reads books of science, though without any desire fixed of improvement, will grow more knowing; he that entertains himself with moral or religious treatises, will imperceptibly advance in goodness; the ideas which are often offered to the mind, will at last find a lucky moment when it is disposed to receive them.

SAMUEL JOHNSON, *The Adventurer*, No. 137

What refuge is there for the victim who is oppressed with the feeling that there are a thousand new books he ought to read, while life is only long enough for him to attempt to read a hundred.

OLIVER WENDELL HOLMES, *Over the Teacups*

To divert at any time a troublesome fancy, run to thy books; they always receive thee with the same kindness.

> THOMAS FULLER, *The Holy and the Profane State*,
> 'Of Books'

Woe be to him that reads but one book.

> GEORGE HERBERT, *Jacula Prudentum*

> *For books are more than books, they are the life*
> *The very heart and core of ages past,*
> *The reason why men lived and worked and died,*
> *The essence and quintessence of their lives.*
>
> AMY LOWELL, *The Boston Athenæum*

Books are not absolutely dead things, but do contain a potency of life in them to be as active as that soul was whose progeny they are; nay they do preserve as in a vial the purest efficacy and extraction of that living intellect that bred them.

> JOHN MILTON, *Areopagitica*

A book that furnishes no quotations is, *me judice*, no book – it is a plaything.

> THOMAS LOVE PEACOCK, *Crotchet Castle*

One advantage there certainly is in quotation, that if the authors cited be good, there is at least so much worth reading in the book of him who quotes them.

> SAMUEL JOHNSON, Quoted in Boswell's *Life of Johnson*

Making books is a skilled trade, like making clocks.

> JEAN DE LA BRUYÈRE, *Les Caractères*

He that publishes a book runs a very great hazard, since nothing can be more impossible than to compose one that may secure the approbation of every reader.

> MIGUEL DE CERVANTES, *Don Quixote*

> *Some said, John, print it; others said,*
> *Not so;*

> *Some said, It might do good; others*
> *said,* No.
>> JOHN BUNYAN, Author's apology for his Book,
>> *The Pilgrim's Progress*

The images of men's wits and knowledges remain in books, exempted from the wrong of time, and capable of perpetual renovation.
>> FRANCIS BACON, *Advancement Of Learning*, Bk. I

There is no such thing as a moral or an immoral book. Books are well written, or badly written. That is all.
>> OSCAR WILDE, *The Picture of Dorian Gray*, Preface

I never knew a girl who was ruined by a book.
>> JAMES J. WALKER, New York Senate Debate on Censorship

Few books have more than one thought: the generality indeed have not quite so many.
>> JULIUS CHARLES HARE and AUGUSTUS WILLIAM HARE
>> *Guesses at Truth*

He hath never fed of the dainties that are bred in a book; he hath not eat paper, as it were; he hath not drunk ink; his intellect is not replenished.
>> WILLIAM SHAKESPEARE, *Love's Labour's Lost*

A classic is produced by the cooperation of the public with the author. A classic is a work which is fit to enter into permanent relations with a large section of mankind.
>> OSCAR W. FIRKINS, *Lecture Notes*

> *Pray thee, take care, that tak'st my book in hand,*
> *To read it well; that is, to understand.*
>> BEN JONSON, *Epigrams*, No. I

> *Here stand my books, line upon line,*
> *They reach the roof, and row by row,*

*They speak of faded tastes of mine,*
*And things I did, but do not, know.*
ANDREW LANG, *Ballade of his Books*

Yon second-hand bookseller is second to none in the worth of the treasures which he dispenses.
JAMES HENRY LEIGH HUNT, *On the Beneficence of Bookstalls*

Where is human nature so weak as in the book-store?
HENRY WARD BEECHER, *Star Papers*, 'Subtleties of Book Buyers'

A presentation copy . . . is a copy of a book which does not sell, sent you by the author, with his foolish autograph at the beginning of it; for which, if a stranger, he only demands your friendship; if a brother author, he expects from you a book of yours, which does not sell, in return.
CHARLES LAMB, *Last Essays of Elia*,
'Popular Fallacies'

I never read a book before reviewing it, it prejudices a man so.
SYDNEY SMITH, *H. Pearson, The Smith of Smiths*

*This books can do – nor this alone: they give*
*New views to life, and teach us how to live;*
*They soothe the grieved, the stubborn they chastise;*
*Fools they admonish, and confirm the wise,*
*Their aid they yield to all: they never shun*
*The man of sorrow, nor the wretch undone;*
*Unlike the hard, the selfish, and the proud,*
*They fly not from the suppliant crowd;*
*Nor tell to various people various things,*
*But show to subjects, what they show to Kings.*
GEORGE CRABBE, *The Library*

*Of writing many books there is no end.*
ELIZABETH BARRETT BROWNING, *Aurora Leigh*

# 2
# Readers and Reading

A man ought to read just as inclination leads him; for what he reads as a task will do him little good.

SAMUEL JOHNSON, Quoted in Boswell's *Life of Johnson*

Of all the human relaxations which are free from guilt, none so dignified as reading.

SIR SAMUEL EGERTON BRYDGES, *The Ruminator*, No. 24

The first time I read an excellent book, it is to me just as if I had gained a new friend: when I read over a book I have perused before, it resembles the meeting with an old one.

OLIVER GOLDSMITH, *Citizen of the World*

Reading is to the mind what exercise is to the body.

SIR RICHARD STEELE, *The Tatler*, No. 147

To read without reflecting, is like eating without digesting.

EDMUND BURKE, *Letters*

Be sure that you go to the author to get at *his* meaning, not to find yours.

JOHN RUSKIN, *Sesame and Lilies*

To read well, that is, to read true books in a true spirit, is a noble exercise.

HENRY DAVID THOREAU, *Walden*, 'Reading'

The delight of opening a new pursuit, or a new course of reading,

imparts the vivacity and novelty of youth, even to old age.
ISAAC D'ISRAELI, *Literary Character of Men of Genius*

It is a tie between men to have read the same book.
RALPH WALDO EMERSON, *Journals*, 1864

If I have not read a book before, it is, to all intents and purposes, new to me, whether it was printed yesterday or three hundred years ago.
WILLIAM HAZLITT, *On Reading New Books*

In reading some books we occupy ourselves chiefly with the thoughts of the author; in perusing others, exclusively with our own.
EDGAR ALLAN POE, *Marginalia*

We read fine things but never feel them to the full until we have gone the same steps as the author.
JOHN KEATS, *Letter to John Hamilton Reynolds*, 1818

Have you ever rightly considered what the mere ability to read means? That it is the key which admits us to the whole world of thought and fancy and imagination? to the company of saint and sage, of the wisest and the wittiest at their wisest and wittiest moment? That it enables us to see with the keenest eyes, hear with the finest ears, and listen to the sweetest voices of all time?
JAMES RUSSELL LOWELL, *Democracy and Other Addresses*,
'Books and Libraries'

There is a great deal of difference between the eager man who wants to read a book, and the tired man who wants a book to read.
G. K. CHESTERTON, *Charles Dickens*

Good literature continually read for pleasure must, let us hope, do some good to the reader.
ALFRED EDWARD HOUSMAN, *The Name and Nature of Poetry*,
Lecture delivered at Cambridge University, 9 May, 1933

Who is he . . . that will not be much lightened in his mind by

reading of some enticing story, true or feigned?
ROBERT BURTON, *Anatomy of Melancholy*,
'Democritus to the Reader'

There is nothing better fitted to delight the reader than change of
circumstances and varieties of fortune.
MARCUS TULLIUS CICERO, *Epistolæ ad Atticum*,
Bk. 5, Epis. 12

The only obligation to which in advance we may hold a novel,
without incurring the accusation of being arbitrary, is that it be
interesting.
HENRY JAMES, *The Art of Fiction*,
'Partial Portraits'

In anything fit to be called by the name of reading, the process itself
should be absorbing and voluptuous; we should gloat over a book,
be rapt clean out of ourselves.
ROBERT LOUIS STEVENSON, *A Gossip on Romance*

Reading is not a duty, and has consequently no business to be made
disagreeable.
AUGUSTINE BIRRELL, *Obiter Dicta*, Second Series,
'The Office of Literature'

All good and true book-lovers practise the pleasing and improving
avocation of reading in bed.
EUGENE FIELD, *Love Affairs of a Bibliomaniac*

Reading furnishes the mind only with materials of knowledge; it is
thinking makes what we read ours.
JOHN LOCKE, *Conduct of Understanding*, 'Reading'

*Learn to read slow: all other graces*
*Will follow in their proper places.*
WILLIAM WALKER, *The Art of Reading*

The works of the great poets have never yet been read by mankind, for only the great poets can read them . . . Most men have learned to read to serve a paltry convenience . . . but of reading as a noble intellectual exercise they know little or nothing.

HENRY DAVID THOREAU, *Walden*, 'Reading'

Our high respect for a well-read man is praise enough of literature.

RALPH WALDO EMERSON, *Letters and Social Aims*, 'Quotation and Originality'

Life being short and the quiet hours of it few, we ought to waste none of them in reading valueless books.

JOHN RUSKIN, *Sesame and Lilies*, Preface

In science, read by preference the newest works; in literature, the oldest. The classics are always modern.

EDWARD BULWER-LYTTON, Baron Lytton, *Caxtoniana*, 'Hints on Mental Culture'

*The mind, relaxing into needful sport,*
*Should turn to writers of an abler sort,*
*Whose wit well manag'd, and whose classic style,*
*Give truth a lustre, and make wisdom smile.*

WILLIAM COWPER, *Retirement*

One of the amusements of idleness is reading without the fatigue of close attention; and the world, therefore, swarms with writers whose wish is not to be studied, but to be read.

SAMUEL JOHNSON, *The Idler*

For what are the classics but the noblest recorded thoughts of man? They are the only oracles which are not decayed.

HENRY DAVID THOREAU, *Walden*, 'Reading'

A classic is something that everybody wants to have read and nobody wants to read.

MARK TWAIN, Speech, *The Disappearance of Literature*

I have confessed to you my utter inability to remember in any comprehensive way what I read. I can vehemently applaud, or perversely stickle, at *parts*; but I cannot grasp at a whole.

CHARLES LAMB, *Letter to Godwin*, 1803

The three practical rules then, which I have to offer, are, – 1. Never read any book that is not a year old. 2. Never read any but famed books. 3. Never read any but what you like.

RALPH WALDO EMERSON, *Society and Solitude*, 'Books'

It is poor travelling that is only to arrive, and it is poor reading that is only to find out how the book ends.

ARTHUR WILLIS COLTON, *The Reader*

The book-worm wraps himself up in his web of verbal generalities, and sees only the glimmering shadows of things reflected from the minds of others.

WILLIAM HAZLITT, *Table Talk*,
'On the Ignorance of the Learned'

> *And better had they ne'er been born*
> *Who read to doubt, or read to scorn.*
> SIR WALTER SCOTT, *The Monastery*

It seems to me much better to read a man's own writing than to read what others say about him, especially when the man is first-rate and the 'others' are third-rate.

GEORGE ELIOT, *Letter to Miss Hennell*, 1865

> *We get no good*
> *By being ungenerous, even to a book,*
> *And calculating profits, – so much help*
> *By so much reading. It is rather when*
> *We gloriously forget ourselves and plunge*
> *Soul-forward, headlong, into a book's profound,*
> *Impassioned for its beauty and salt of truth –*
> *'Tis then we get the right good from a book.*
> ELIZABETH BARRETT BROWNING, *Aurora Leigh*

Some read to think, – these are rare; some to write, – these are common; and some to talk, – and these form the great majority.

CHARLES CALEB COLTON, *Lacon*

There is an art of reading, as well as an art of thinking, and an art of writing.

ISAAC D'ISRAELI, *Lit ·ary Character*

Example is a lesson that all men can read.

GILBERT WEST, *Education*

Reading maketh a full man; conference a ready man; and writing an exact man.

FRANCIS BACON, *Essays*, 'Of Studies'

Who often reads will sometimes wish to write.

GEORGE CRABBE, *Tales*, 'Edward Shore'

Every book is worth reading which sets the reader in a working mood.

RALPH WALDO EMERSON, *Uncollected Lectures*, 'Resources'

People say that life is the thing, but I prefer reading.

LOGAN PEARSALL SMITH, *Afterthoughts*

I never travel without my diary. One should always have something sensational to read in the train.

OSCAR WILDE, *The Importance of Being Earnest*

# 3
# Writers

The two most engaging powers of an author are to make *new* things *familiar*, and *familiar* things *new*.

SAMUEL JOHNSON, *Lives of the Poets*, 'Pope'

His (Sir Walter Scott's) works – taken together – are almost like a new edition of human nature. This is indeed to be an author!

WILLIAM HAZLITT, *English Literature*, Sir Walter Scott

Rudyard Kipling is a stranger to me but he is a most remarkable man – and I am the other one. Between us we cover all knowledge; he knows all that can be known and I know the rest.

MARK TWAIN, *Autobiography*

> *Whatever the word* great *means,*
> *Charles Dickens was what it means.*

G. K. CHESTERTON, *Preface to Dickens's Pickwick Papers*

I approve Mr Thackeray. This may sound presumptuous perhaps, but I mean that I have long recognized in his writings genuine talent, such as I admired, such as I wondered at and delighted in. No author seems to distinguish so exquisitely as he does dross from ore, the real from the counterfeit.

CHARLOTTE BRONTË, On William Makepeace Thackeray in *Letter to W. S. Williams*, 28 October 1847

While an author is yet living, we estimate his powers by his worst performance; and when he is dead, we rate them by his best.

SAMUEL JOHNSON, *Works*

And, after all, it is style alone by which posterity will judge of a great work, for an author can have nothing truly his own but his style.

ISAAC D'ISRAELI, *Literary Miscellanies*, 'Style'

The most original authors of modern times are so, not because they create anything new, but only because they are able to say things in a manner as if they had never been said before.

JOHANN WOLFGANG VON GOETHE, *Sprüche in Prosa*, 1819

> *Our author by experience finds it true,*
> *'Tis much more hard to please himself than you.*
>
> JOHN DRYDEN, *Aureng-Zebe, Prologue*

Choose an author as you choose a friend.

WENTWORTH DILLON, EARL OF ROSCOMMON,
*Essay on Translated Verse*

The faults of great authors are generally excellencies carried to excess.

SAMUEL TAYLOR COLERIDGE, *Miscellanies*

A man may be a very good author with some faults, but not with many faults.

FRANÇOIS MARIE AROUET VOLTAIRE, *Letters on the English*

The circumstance which gives authors an advantage above all these great masters, is this, that they can multiply their originals; or rather, can make copies of their works, to what number they please, which shall be as valuable as the originals themselves.

JOSEPH ADDISON, *The Spectator*, No. 166

They lard their lean books with the fat of others' works.

ROBERT BURTON, *Anatomy of Melancholy*,
'Democritus to the Reader'

Nothing gives an author so much pleasure as to find his works respectfully quoted by other learned authors.

BENJAMIN FRANKLIN, *Pennsylvania Almanac,*
'Poor Richard's Almanac'

The praise of ancient authors proceeds not from the reverence of the dead, but from the competition and mutual envy of the living.

THOMAS HOBBES, *Leviathan*

For several days after my first book was published I carried it about in my pocket, and took surreptitious peeps at it to make sure that the ink had not faded.

SIR JAMES MATTHEW BARRIE, *Speech at the Critics' Circle,*
*London,* 1922

He was a one-book man. Some men have only one book in them; others, a library.

SYDNEY SMITH, *Lady Holland, Memoir*

> *One hates an author that's all author, fellows*
> *In foolscap uniforms turn'd up with ink,*
> *So very anxious, clever, fine, and jealous,*
> *One don't know what to say to them, or think,*
> *Unless to puff them with a pair of bellows.*
>
> LORD BYRON, *Beppo*

The only happy author in this world is he who is below the care of reputation.

WASHINGTON IRVING, *Tales of a Traveller,*
'Poor-Devil Author'

Authors have established it as a kind of rule, that a man ought to be dull sometimes; as the most severe reader makes allowances for many rests and nodding-places in a voluminous writer.

JOSEPH ADDISON, *The Spectator,* No. 124

I consider an author's literary reputation to be alive only while his name will insure a good price for his copy from the booksellers.

OLIVER GOLDSMITH, Quoted in Boswell's *Life of Johnson*

What I like in a good author is not what he says, but what he whispers.

> LOGAN PEARSALL SMITH, *Afterthoughts*

An author ought to write for the youth of his own generation, the critics of the next, and the schoolmasters of ever afterwards.

> F. SCOTT FITZGERALD, *Quoted in The Guardian*, 1964

There is probably no hell for authors in the next world – they suffer so much from critics and publishers in this.

> CHRISTIAN NESTELL BOVEE, *Summaries of Thought*, 'Authors'

Authors are like cattle going to a fair: those of the same field can never move on without butting one another.

> WALTER SAVAGE LANDOR, *Imaginary Conversations*,
> 'Archdeacon Hare and Walter Landor'

I think I may boast myself to be, with all possible vanity, the most unlearned and uninformed female who ever dared to be an authoress.

> JANE AUSTEN, *Letter to the Rev. James Clarke*, 1815

Whatever may be the success of my stories, I shall be resolute in preserving my incognito, having observed that a *nom de plume* secures all the advantages without the disagreeables of reputation.

> GEORGE ELIOT, *Letter to John Blackwood*, 1857

I have seen so little of the world that I have nothing but thin air to concoct my stories of, and it is not easy to give a life-like semblance to such shadowy stuff.

> NATHANIEL HAWTHORNE, *Letter to Henry Wadsworth Longfellow*, 1838

I met Sir Bulwer Lytton, or Lytton Bulwer. He is anxious about some scheme for some association of literary men. I detest all such associations. I hate the notion of gregarious authors. The less we have to do with each other the better.

> LORD MACAULAY, *Life and Letters of Lord Macaulay*

I don't want to be a doctor, and live by men's diseases; nor a minister to live by their sins; nor a lawyer to live by their quarrels. So I don't see there's anything left for me but to be an author.

NATHANIEL HAWTHORNE, *Remark to his Mother*

A man starts upon a sudden, takes Pen, Ink, and Paper, and without ever having had a thought of it before, resolves within himself he will write a Book; he has no Talent at Writing, but he wants fifty Guineas.

JEAN DE LA BRUYÈRE, *Les Caractères*

> *An author! 'tis a venerable name!*
> *How few deserve it, and what numbers claim!*
> EDWARD YOUNG, *Epistles to Mr Pope*

I am always at a loss to know how much to believe of my own stories.

WASHINGTON IRVING, *Tales of a Traveller*,
'To the Reader'

An author who speaks about his own books is almost as bad as a mother who talks about her own children.

BENJAMIN DISRAELI, Speech, Glasgow, 1873

I shall be but a shrimp of an author.

THOMAS GRAY, *Letter to Horace Walpole*, 1768

Young Author: Yes, Agassiz *does* recommend authors to eat fish, because the phosphorus in it makes brains. But I cannot help you to a decision about the amount you need to eat. Perhaps a couple of whales would be enough.

MARK TWAIN, *Sketches*, 'Answers to Correspondents'

> *The readers and the hearers like my books,*
> *But yet some writers cannot them digest;*
> *But what care I? for when I make a feast*
> *I would my guests should praise it, not the cooks.*
> SIR JOHN HARINGTON, *Epigrams*, 'Of Writers who
> Carp at other Men's Books'

That writer does the most, who gives his reader the *most* knowledge, and takes from him the *least* time.

CHARLES CALEB COLTON, *Lacon*, Preface

The ablest writer is a gardener first, and then a cook. His tasks are, carefully to select and cultivate his strongest and most nutritive thoughts, and, when they are ripe, to dress them wholesomely, and so that they may have a relish.

JULIUS CHARLES HARE and AUGUSTUS WILLIAM HARE,
*Guesses at Truth*

Writers, like teeth, are divided into incisors and grinders.

WALTER BAGEHOT, *Literary Studies*,
'The First Edinburgh Reviewers'

The writer, like the priest, must be exempted from secular labor. His works needs a frolic health; he must be at the top of his condition.

RALPH WALDO EMERSON, *Poetry and Imagination*

Every habit and faculty is confirmed and strengthened by the corresponding actions, that of walking by walking, that of running by running. If you wish to be a good reader, read; if you wish to be a good writer, write.

EPICTETUS, *Discourses*

It is a hard and nice thing for a man to write of himself. It grates his own heart to say anything of disparagement, and the reader's ears to hear anything of praise from him.

ABRAHAM COWLEY, *Of Myself*

The original writer is not he who refrains from imitating others, but he who can be imitated by none.

FRANÇOIS RENE DE CHATEAUBRIAND, *Génie du Christianisme*

'Tis a vanity common to all writers, to over-value their own productions.

JOHN DRYDEN, *Examen Poeticum*, Dedication

He, with his copy-rights and copy-wrongs, in his squalid garret, in his rusty coat; ruling (for this is what he does), from his grave, after death, whole nations and generations who would, or would not, give him bread while living, – is a rather curious spectacle!

> THOMAS CARLYLE, *On Heroes and Hero-Worship*,
> 'The Hero as Man of Letters'

Thou art a retailer of phrases, and dost deal in remnants of remnants.

> WILLIAM CONGREVE, *The Way of the World*

I never desire to converse with a man who has written more than he has read.

> SAMUEL JOHNSON, *Miscellanies*, Vol. 2

Miscellanists are the most popular writers among every people; for it is they who form a communication between the learned and the unlearned, and, as it were, throw a bridge between those two great divisions of the public.

> ISAAC D'ISRAELI, *Literary Character of*
> *Men of Genius*, 'Miscellanists'

One writer, for instance, excels at a plan or a title page, another works away the body of the book, and a third is a dab at an index.

> OLIVER GOLDSMITH, *The Bee*, No. 1, 6 October, 1759

I have often thought that a story-teller is born, as well as a poet.

> SIR RICHARD STEELE, *The Guardian*, No. 42

Until you understand a writer's ignorance, presume yourself ignorant of his understanding.

> SAMUEL TAYLOR COLERIDGE, *Biographia Literaria*

The man must have a fair recipe for melancholy, who can be dull in Fleet Street.

> CHARLES LAMB, *The Londoner* in letter
> to Thomas Manning, 1802

# 4
# Writing

When once the itch of literature comes over a man, nothing can cure it but the scratching of a pen.

SAMUEL LOVER, *Handy Andy*

I would rather be Charles Lamb than Charles XII. I would rather be remembered by a song than by a victory. I would rather build a fine sonnet than have built St Paul's . . . Fine phrases I value more than bank-notes. I have ear for no other harmony than the harmony of words.

ALEXANDER SMITH, *Dreamthorp*, 'Men of Letters'

Arts and sciences are not cast in a mould, but are found and perfected by degrees, by often handling and polishing, as bears leisurely lick their cubs into shape.

MICHEL DE MONTAIGNE, *Essays*, Bk. 2

Every man's work, whether it be literature or music or pictures or architecture or anything else, is always a portrait of himself, and the more he tries to conceal himself the more clearly will his character appear in spite of him.

SAMUEL BUTLER, *The Way of all Felsh*

Whatever an author puts between the two covers of his book is public property; whatever of himself he does not put there is his private property, as much as if he had never written a word.

GAIL HAMILTON, *Country Living and Country Thinking*,
Preface

When I put down Mr Johnson's Sayings, I do not keep strictly to chronology. I am glad to collect the gold dust, as I get by degrees as much as will be an ingot.

JAMES BOSWELL, *On Dr Samuel Johnson*,
Journal, 14 April, 1775

A great writer creates a world of his own and his readers are proud to live in it. A lesser writer may entice them in for a moment, but soon he will watch them filing out.

CYRIL CONNOLLY, *Enemies of Promise*

All good writing is *swimming under water* and holding your breath.

F. SCOTT FITZGERALD, *Letter to Frances Scott Fitzgerald*

Good writing is a kind of skating which carries off the performer where he would not go.

RALPH WALDO EMERSON, *Journals*, Vol. 7

Writing, when properly managed (as you may be sure I think mine is), is but a different name for conversation.

LAURENCE STERNE, *Tristram Shandy*

It is my ambition to say in ten sentences what everyone else says in a whole book, – what everyone else does *not* say in a whole book.

FRIEDRICH WILHELM NIETZSCHE, *Skirmishes in a
War with the Age*

> *For words, like Nature, half reveal*
> *And half conceal the Soul within.*
> ALFRED LORD TENNYSON, *In Memoriam*, Prologue

Next to the originator of a good sentence is the first quoter of it.

RALPH WALDO EMERSON, *Letters and Social Aims*,
'Quotation and Originality'

Fine art is that in which the hand, the head, and the heart of man go together.

JOHN RUSKIN, *The Two Paths*

The excellence of every art is its intensity, capable of making all disagreeables evaporate, from their being in close relationship with beauty and truth.

JOHN KEATS, *Letter to G. and T. Keats*, 1817

How long a time lies in one little word!

WILLIAM SHAKESPEARE, *King Richard II*

A work that aspires, however humbly, to the condition of art should carry its justification in every line.

JOSEPH CONRAD, *The Nigger and the Narcissus*, Preface

*Dear authors! suit your topics to your strength,*
*And ponder well your subject and its length.*

LORD BYRON, *Hints from Horace*

The test of a vocation is the love of the drudgery it involves.

LOGAN PEARSALL SMITH, *Afterthoughts*

Let there be gall enough in thy ink, though thou wrote with a goose-pen, no matter.

WILLIAM SHAKESPEARE, *Twelfth Night*

Ready writing makes not good writing; but good writing brings on ready writing.

BEN JONSON, *Explorata*, 'De Stylo'

If one has no heart, one cannot write for the masses.

HEINRICH HEINE, *Letter to Julius Campe*, 1840

My real judgement of my own work is that I have spoilt a number of jolly good ideas in my time.

G. K. CHESTERTON, *Autobiography*

*Whate'er is well-conceived is clearly said,*
*And the words to say it flow with ease.*

NICHOLAS BOILEAU-DESPRÉAUX, *L'Art Poétique*

*Of all the arts in which the wise excel,*
*Nature's chief masterpiece is writing well.*
JOHN SHEFFIELD, DUKE OF BUCKINGHAM AND NORMANBY,
*Essay on Poetry*

Learn to write well, or not to write at all.
JOHN DRYDEN and JOHN SHEFFIELD, DUKE OF BUCKINGHAM
AND NORMANBY, *An Essay upon Satire*

Words are the only things that last forever.
WILLIAM HAZLITT, *Table Talk*, 'On Thought and Action'

*But words are things; and a small drop of ink,*
*Falling, like dew, upon a thought, produces*
*That which makes thousands, perhaps millions, think.*
LORD BYRON, *Don Juan*

When I write in a Hurry I always feel to be not worth reading, and
what I try to take Pains with, I am sure never to finish . . .
RICHARD BRINSLEY SHERIDAN, Letter to David Garrick,
10 January, 1778

By words the mind is excited and the spirit elated.
ARISTOPHANES, *The Birds*

Words are like money; there is nothing so useless, unless when in
actual use.
SAMUEL BUTLER, *Note Books*, 'On the Making of Music,
Pictures and Books'

It is extremely natural for us to desire to see such our thoughts put
into the dress of words, without which indeed we can scarce have a
clear and distinct idea of them our selves.
EUSTACE BUDGELL, *The Spectator*, No. 379

Words have weight, sound and appearance; it is only by considering

these that you can write a sentence that is good to look at and good to
listen to.

SOMERSET MAUGHAM, *The Summing Up*

Elegance in prose composition is mainly this: A just admission of
topics and of words; neither too many nor too few of either; enough
of sweetness in the sound to induce us to enter and sit still; enough of
illustration and reflection to change the posture of our minds when
they would tire; and enough of sound matter in the complex to repay
us for our attendance.

WALTER SAVAGE LANDOR, *Imaginary Conversations*,
'Chesterfield and Chatham'

To sing the same tune, as the saying is, is in everything cloying and
offensive; but men are generally pleased with variety.

PLUTARCH, *Of the Training of Children*

How many honest words have suffered corruption since Chaucer's
days!

THOMAS MIDDLETON, *No Wit, No Help, Like a Woman's*

> *Men ever had, and ever will have, leave*
> *To coin new words well suited to the age.*
> *Words are like leaves, some wither ev'ry year,*
> *And ev'ry year a younger race succeeds.*

HORACE, *Ars Poetica*

Words are the small change of thought.

JULES RENARD, *Journal*, November 1888

I hate false words, and seek with care, difficulty, and moroseness,
those that fit the thing.

WALTER SAVAGE LANDOR, *Imaginary Conversations*,
Bishop Burnet and Humphrey Hardcastle'

Words are, of course, the most powerful drug used by mankind.

RUDYARD KIPLING, Speech, 1923

Every word that is superfluous flows away from the full mind.

HORACE, *Ars Poetica*

Few were his words, but wonderfully clear.

HOMER, *Iliad*

Good words are worth much and cost little.

GEORGE HERBERT, *Jacula Prudentum*

The pen is the tongue of the mind.

MIGUEL DE CERVANTES, *Don Quixote*

> *You write with ease, to show your breeding,*
> *But easy writing's vile hard reading.*
>
> RICHARD BRINSLEY SHERIDAN, *Clio's Protest*

The secret of all good writing is sound judgment.

HORACE, *Ars Poetica*

The dialogue of this author is often so evidently determined by the incident which produces it, and is pursued with so much ease and simplicity, that it seems scarcely to claim the merit of fiction, but to have been gleaned by diligent selection out of common conversation, and common occurrences.

SAMUEL JOHNSON, *Preface to the Plays of William Shakespeare*

The ancients wrote at a time when the great art of writing badly had not yet been invented. In those days to write at all meant to write well.

G. C. LICHTENBERG, *Reflections*

Knowledge is the foundation and source of good writing.

HORACE, *Ars Poetica*

I am convinced more and more every day that fine writing is, next to fine doing, the top thing in the world.

JOHN KEATS, *Letter to J. H. Reynolds*, 1819

I'll call for pen and ink, and write my mind.
WILLIAM SHAKESPEARE, *Henry VI*

> *A mediocre mind thinks it writes divinely;*
> *A good mind thinks it writes reasonably.*
> JEAN DE LA BRUYÈRE, *Charactères*

Articulate words are a harsh clamor and dissonance. When man arrives at his highest perfection, he will again be dumb!
NATHANIEL HAWTHORNE, *American Note Books*, April, 1841

There are favorable hours for reading a book, as for writing it.
HENRY WADSWORTH LONGFELLOW, *Table Talk*

Whatever is felicitously expressed risks being worse expressed: it is a wretched taste to be gratified with mediocrity when the excellent lies before us.
ISAAC D'ISRAELI, *Curiosities of Literature*, 'On Quotation'

Seek what to write, rather than how to write it.
SENECA, *Ad Lucilium*

Choose a subject, ye who write, suited to your strength.
HORACE, *Ars Poetica*

Never write on a subject without having first read yourself full on it; and never read on a subject 'till you have thought yourself hungry on it.
JEAN PAUL RICHTER, *Hesperus*

Now, what I want is Facts. . . . Facts alone are wanted in life.
CHARLES DICKENS, *Hard Times*

You will find it a very good practice always to verify your references, sir!
MARTIN JESEPH ROUTH, Attributed

He listens well who takes notes.

DANTE, *The Divine Comedy*, 'Inferno'

What is the use of brevity if it constitutes a book?

MARTIAL, *Epigrams*, Bk. 8

Write what will sell! To this Golden Rule every minor canon must be subordinate.

EDWARD COPLESTON, *Advice to a Young Reviewer*

What we have to learn to do, we learn by doing.

ARISTOTLE, *Ethics*

Our admiration of fine writing will always be in proportion to its real difficulty and its apparent ease.

CHARLES CALEB COLTON, *Lacon*

Writing is not literature unless it gives to the reader a pleasure which arises not only from the things said, but from the way in which they are said.

STOPFORD A. BROOKE, *Primer of English Literature*

To achieve a racy narrative, thin the words down.

ANON

Who casts to write a living line, must sweat.

BEN JONSON, *To the Memory of William Shakespeare*

Whatever is worth doing at all, is worth doing well.

LORD CHESTERFIELD, *Letter to his son*, 1746

Practice is the best of all instruction.

PUBILIUS SYRUS, *Maxim* 439

In composing, as a general rule, run your pen through every other word you have written; you have no idea what vigor it will give your style.

SYDNEY SMITH, *Lady Holland, Memoir*

An old tutor of a college said to one of his pupils: Read over your compositions, and wherever you meet with a passage which you think is particularly fine, strike it out.

SAMUEL JOHNSON, Quoted in Boswell's *Life of Johnson*

> *Little do such men know the toil, the pains,*
> *The daily, nightly racking of the brains,*
> *To range the thoughts, the matter to digest,*
> *To cull fit phrases, and reject the rest.*
>
> CHARLES CHURCHILL, *Gotham*

When a man is in doubt about this or that in his writing, it will often guide him if he asks himself how it will tell a hundred years hence.

SAMUEL BUTLER, *Note Books*

For the creation of a master-work of literature two powers must concur, the power of the man and the power of the moment.

MATTHEW ARNOLD, *The Function of Criticism*

Literature is strewn with the wreckage of men who have minded beyond reason the opinion of others.

VIRGINIA WOOLF, *A Room of One's Own*

He that uses many words for the explaining any subject, doth, like the cuttle fish, hide himself for the most part in his own ink.

JOHN RAY, *On the Creation*

Whatever you teach, be brief, that your readers' minds may readily comprehend and faithfully retain your words. Everything superfluous slips from the full heart.

HORACE, *Ars Poetica*

> *Words are like leaves; and where they most abound,*
> *Much fruit of sense beneath is rarely found.*
>
> ALEXANDER POPE, *Essay on Criticism*

Many writers profess great exactness in punctuation, who never yet made a point.

GEORGE DENNISON PRENTICE, Prenticeana

I think that too many (punctuation) stops stop the way, and that every sixth or seventh is uncalled for.

WALTER SAVAGE LANDOR, Letter to John Forster

As to the Adjective: when in doubt, strike it out.

MARK TWAIN, Pudd'nhead Wilson's Calendar

There can be no doubt that the best method of writing is to lay our literary compositions aside for a while, that we may after a reasonable period return to them, and find them, as it were, altogether new to us.

MARCUS QUINTILIAN, De Institutione Oratoria

> *Blot out, correct, insert, refine,*
> *Enlarge, diminish, interline;*
> *Be mindful, when invention fails,*
> *To scratch your head, and bite your nails.*

JONATHAN SWIFT, On Poetry

Often you must turn your stylus to erase, if you hope to write something worth a second reading.

HORACE, Satires

> *Whatever hath been written shall remain,*
> *Nor be erased nor written o'er again,*
> *The unwritten only still belongs to thee:*
> *Take heed, and ponder well what that shall be.*

HENRY WADSWORTH LONGFELLOW, Morituri Salutamus

> *True ease in writing comes from art, not chance,*
> *As those move easiest who have learn'd to dance.*
> *'Tis not enough no harshness gives offence,*
> *The sound must seem an echo to the sense.*

ALEXANDER POPE, An Essay on Criticism

Once a word has been allowed to escape, it cannot be recalled.
HORACE, *Epistles*

To profit from good advice requires more wisdom than to give it.
JOHN CHURTON COLLINS, *Aphorisms*

*Of every noble work the silent part is best,*
*Of all expression that which can not be expressed.*
WILLIAM WETMORE STORY, *The Unexpressed*

The book that he has made renders its author this service in return,
that so long as the book survives, its author remains immortal and
cannot die.
RICHARD DE BURY, *Philobiblon*

To make a book is as much a trade as to make a clock; something
more than intelligence is required to become an author.
JEAN DE LA BRUYÈRE, *Caractères*

Satire is a sort of glass, wherein beholders do generally discover
everybody's face but their own.
JONATHAN SWIFT, *The Battle of the Books*

Everyone has a mass of bad work in him which he will have to work
off and get rid of before he can do better – and indeed, the more
lasting a man's ultimate good work, the more sure he is to pass
through a time, and perhaps a very long one, in which there seems
very little hope for him at all. We must all sow our spiritual wild
oats.
SAMUEL BUTLER, *The Way of All Flesh*

Composition is, for the most part, an effort of slow diligence and
steady perseverance, to which the mind is dragged by necessity or
resolution.
SAMUEL JOHNSON, *The Adventurer*, No. 138

Blessed is the man who, having nothing to say, abstains from giving in words evidence of the fact.

GEORGE ELIOT, *Impressions of Theophrastus Such*

When a dog bites a man that is not news, but when a man bites a dog that is news.

CHARLES ANDERSON DANA, 'What is News?',
*The New York Sun*, 1882

The nature of bad news infects the teller.

WILLIAM SHAKESPEARE, *Antony and Cleopatra*

Every man is a borrower and a mimic, life is theatrical and literature a quotation.

RALPH WALDO EMERSON, *Society and Solitude*, 'Success'

If it be true that 'good wine needs no bush,' 'tis true that a good play needs no epilogue.

WILLIAM SHAKESPEARE, *As You Like It*

I like writing with a Peacock's Quill; because its Feathers are all Eyes.

THOMAS FULLER, *Gnomologia*

I knew one, that when he wrote a letter, he would put that which was most material, in the Post-script, as if it had been a by-matter.

FRANCIS BACON, *Essays*, 'Of Cunning'

Considering the multitude of mortals that handle the pen in these days, and can mostly spell, and write without glaring violations of grammar, the question naturally arises: How is it, then, that no work proceeds from them, bearing any stamp of authenticity and permanence; of worth for more than one day?

THOMAS CARLYLE, *Biography*

A well-written Life is almost as rare as a well-spent one.

THOMAS CARLYLE, *Critical and Miscellaneous Essays*, 'Richter'

*With pen and pencil we're learning to say*
*Nothing, more cleverly every day.*
WILLIAM ALLINGHAM, *Blackberries*

*The Moving Finger writes; and, having writ*
*Moves on: nor all thy Piety nor Wit*
*Shall lure it back to cancel half a Line,*
*Nor all thy Tears wash out a Word of it.*
EDWARD FITZGERALD, *Rubáiyát of Omar Khayyám*

Consider the postage stamp: its usefulness consists in the ability to stick to one thing till it gets there.
JOSH BILLINGS, *Josh Billings: His Sayings*

'That's rather a sudden pull up, ain't it, Sammy?' inquired Mr Weller.
'Not a bit on it,' said Sam; 'she'll vish there wos more, and that's the great art o' letter writin.'
CHARLES DICKENS, *Pickwick Papers*

Originality is undetected plagiarism.
DEAN WILLIAM RALPH INGE, *Wit and Wisdom*, Preface

*'Tis not how well an author says,*
*But 'tis how much, that gathers praise.*
MATTHEW PRIOR, *Epistle to Fleetwood Shepherd* No. 1

If you would not be forgotten, as soon as you are dead and rotten, either write things worth reading, or do things worth the writing.
BENJAMIN FRANKLIN, *Poor Richard*

*You must lie upon the daisies and discourse*
*in novel phrases of your complicated state of mind,*
*The meaning doesn't matter if it's only*
*idle chatter of a transcendental kind.*
*And everyone will say,*
*As you walk your mystic way,*
*'If this young man expresses himself in*
*terms too deep for me,*

*Why, what a very singularly deep young man*
*this deep young man must be!'*

SIR WILLIAM SCHWENCK GILBERT, *Patience*

Nothing is ended with honour which does not conclude better than it began.

SAMUEL JOHNSON, *The Rambler*, No. 207

*What makes all doctrines plain and clear?*
*About two hundred pounds a year.*
*And that which was prov'd true before,*
*Prove false again? Two hundred more.*

SAMUEL BUTLER, *Hudibras*

There are two things which I am confident I can do very well: one is an introduction to any literary work, stating what it is to contain, and how it should be executed in the most perfect manner; the other is a conclusion, shewing from various causes why the execution has not been equal to what the author promised to himself and to the public.

SAMUEL JOHNSON, Quoted in Boswell's *Life of Johnson*

It is very pleasant to be written up, even by a writer.

JOYCE CARY, *The Horse's Mouth*

Honest John (Bunyan) was the first that I know of who mixed narration and dialogue; a method of writing very engaging to the reader.

BENJAMIN FRANKLIN, *Autobiography*

Truth is a good dog; but beware of barking too close to the heels of an error, lest you get your brains kicked out.

SAMUEL TAYLOR COLERIDGE, *Table Talk*

He has produced a couplet. When our friend is delivered of a couplet, with infinite labour and pain, he takes to his bed, has straw laid down, the knocker tied up, and expects his friends to call and make inquiries.

SYDNEY SMITH, *Lady Holland, Memoir*

The art of writing things that shall sound right and yet be wrong has made so many reputations and afforded comfort to such a large number of readers that I could not venture to neglect it.

SAMUEL BUTLER, *Erewhon*

O what an endless work have I in hand!

EDMUND SPENSER, *Faerie Queene*, Bk. 4

You see what will happen to you if you keep on biting your nails.

SIR NOEL COWARD, Written on a postcard containing a photograph
of the Venus de Milo

All great men have written proudly, nor cared to explain. They knew that the intelligent reader would come at last, and would thank them.

RALPH WALDO EMERSON, *Natural History of Intellect*,
'Thoughts on Modern Literature'

It is very hard to go beyond your public. If they are satisfied with your poor performance, you will not easily make it better.

RALPH WALDO EMERSON, *Journals*, Vol. 9

The only people who can be excused for letting a bad book loose on the world are the poor devils who have to write for a living!

MOLIÈRE, *The Misanthrope*

Indignation at literary wrongs I leave to men born under happier stars. I cannot afford it.

SAMUEL TAYLOR COLERIDGE, *Biographia Literaria*

I never saw an author in my life, saving perhaps one, that did not purr as audibly as a full-grown domestic cat on having his fur smoothed the right way by a skilful hand.

OLIVER WENDELL HOLMES, *The Autocrat of the Breakfast Table*

The fondness for writing grows with writing.

ERASMUS, *Adagia*

The more a man writes, the more he can write.
WILLIAM HAZLITT, *Lectures on Dramatic Literature*, 1820

Think nothing done while aught remains to do.
SAMUEL ROGERS, *Human Life*

A man may write at any time, if he will set himself doggedly to it.
SAMUEL JOHNSON, Quoted in Boswell's *Life of Johnson*

Every man loves what he is good at.
THOMAS SHADWELL, *A True Widow*

Sey forth thy tale, and tarry not the time.
GEOFFREY CHAUCER, *The Reve's Prologue*

The high prize of life, the crowning fortune of a man, is to be born with a bias to some pursuit which finds him in employment and happiness.
RALPH WALDO EMERSON, *Conduct of Life*,
Considerations by the Way'

Against the disease of writing one must take special precautions, since it is a dangerous and contagious disease.
PETER ABELARD, *Letter to Héloise*

> *If all the trees in all the woods were men,*
> *And each and every blade of grass a pen;*
> *If every leaf of every shrub and tree*
> *Turned to a sheet of foolscap; every sea*
> *Were changed to ink, and all the earth's living tribes*
> *Had nothing else to do but act as scribes,*
> *And for ten thousand ages, day and night,*
> *The human race should write, and write, and write,*
> *Till all the pens and paper were used up,*
> *And the huge inkstand was an empty cup,*
> *Still would the scribblers clustered round its brink*
> *Call for more pens, more paper, and more ink.*
> OLIVER WENDELL HOLMES, *Cacoëthes Scribendi*

There is no measure or limit to this fever for writing; every one must be an author; Some out of vanity to acquire celebrity and raise up a name, others for the sake of lucre and gain.

MARTIN LUTHER, *Table Talk*

No man but a blockhead ever wrote except for money.

SAMUEL JOHNSON, Quoted in Boswell's *Life of Johnson*

He wins every hand who mingles profit with pleasure, by delighting and instructing the reader at the same time.

HORACE, *Ars Poetica*

He is well paid that is well satisfied.

WILLIAM SHAKESPEARE, *The Merchant of Venice*

There are few ways in which a man can be more innocently employed than in getting money.

SAMUEL JOHNSON, Quoted in Boswell's *Life of Johnson*

As soon as any art is pursued with a view to money, then farewell, in ninety-nine cases out of a hundred, all hope of genuine good work.

SAMUEL BUTLER, *Note Books*

The impulse to create beauty is rather rare in literary men . . . Far ahead of it comes the yearning to make money. And after the yearning to make money comes the yearning to make a noise.

HENRY LOUIS MENCKEN, *Prejudices*

. . . you must not suppose, because I am a man of letters, that I have never tried to earn an honest living.

GEORGE BERNARD SHAW, *The Irrational Knot*, Preface

# Opportunity

A man must make his opportunity, as oft as find it.

FRANCIS BACON, *Advancement of Learning*, 'Civil Knowledge'

No one knows what he can do till he tries.

PUBILIUS SYRUS, *Maxim 786*

Our chief want in life is somebody who shall make us do what we can.

RALPH WALDO EMERSON, *Conduct of Life*,
'Considerations by the Way'

To the timid and hesitating everything is impossible because it seems so.

SIR WALTER SCOTT, *Rob Roy*

Self-confidence is the first requisite to great undertakings.

SAMUEL JOHNSON, *Works*

All things are difficult before they are easy.

THOMAS FULLER, *Gnomologia*

Nothing, unless it is difficult, is worth while.

OVID, *Ars Amatoria*

Lack of confidence is not the result of difficulty; the difficulty comes from lack of confidence.

SENECA, *Epistulæ ad Lucilium*

> *There is a tide in the affairs of men,*
> *Which, taken at the flood, leads on to fortune;*
> *Omitted, all the voyages of their life*
> *Is bound in shallows and in miseries:*
> *On such a full sea we are now afloat,*
> *And we must take the current when it serves,*
> *Or lose our ventures.*

WILLIAM SHAKESPEARE, *Julius Caesar*

How often things occur by the merest chance, which we dared not even hope for!

TERENCE, *Phormio*

Every one lives by selling something.
ROBERT LOUIS STEVENSON, *Across the Plains*, 'Beggars'

When one door is shut, another opens.
MIGUEL DE CERVANTES, *Don Quixote*

*Nor deem the irrevocable Past,*
*As wholly wasted, wholly vain,*
*If, rising on its wrecks, at last*
*To something nobler we attain.*
HENRY WADSWORTH LONGFELLOW, *Ladder of St Augustine*

*Four things come not back:*
*The spoken word; The sped arrow;*
*Time past; The neglected opportunity.*
OMAR IBN AL-KHATTAB, *Sayings*

He who never fails will never grow rich.
CHARLES HADDON SPURGEON, *John Ploughman*

The man who makes no mistakes does not usually make anything.
EDWARD JOHN PHELPS, Speech at the Mansion House,
London, 1899

To be a well-favoured man is the gift of fortune; but to write and read comes by nature.
WILLIAM SHAKESPEARE, *Much Ado About Nothing*

A wise man will make more opportunities than he finds.
FRANCIS BACON, *Essays*, 'Of Ceremonies and Respects'

Nothing great was ever achieved without enthusiasm.
RALPH WALDO EMERSON, *Essays*, Frist Series, 'Circles'

When the going gets tough, the tough get going!
ANON

If life had a second edition, how I would correct the proofs!

> JOHN CLARE, *Letter to a Friend*

The greatest evil which fortune can inflict on men is to endow them with small talents and great ambition.

> MARQUIS DE LUC DE CLAPIERS VAUVENARGUES,
> *Reflections and Maxims*

If you aspire to the highest place it is no disgrace to stop at the second, or even the third.

> MARCUS TULLIUS CICERO, *De Oratore*

## Beginning

The last thing one discovers in writing a book is what to put first.

> BLAISE PASCAL, *Pensées*

I do not know how to begin.

> LADY MARY WORTLEY MONTAGU, *Letters*, c.1762

My way is to begin with the beginning.

> LORD BYRON, *Don Juan*

So long as a man imagines that he cannot do this or that, so long is he determined not to do it: and consequently, so long it is impossible to him that he should do it.

> BENEDICT SPINOZA, *Ethics*, 'Explanation'

A bad beginning makes a bad ending.

> EURIPIDES, *Aeolus*

A hard beginning maketh a good ending.

> JOHN HEYWOOD, *Proverbs*

The beginning is the most important part of the work.

> PLATO, *The Republic*, Bk. 2

You begin well in nothing except you end well.

THOMAS FULLER, *Gnomologia*

Great is the art of beginning, but greater the art is of ending.

HENRY WADSWORTH LONGFELLOW, *Elegiac Verse*

You may delay, but time will not.

BENJAMIN FRANKLIN, *Poor Richard*

Skill to do comes of doing.

RALPH WALDO EMERSON, *Society and Solitude*: 'Old Age'

In creating, the only hard thing's to begin; A grass-blade's no easier to make than an oak; If you've once found the way, you've achieved the grand stroke.

JAMES RUSSELL LOWELL, *A Fable for Critics*

Nothing is achieved before it be thoroughly attempted.

SIR PHILIP SIDNEY, *Arcadia*

I make a blot upon the paper and begin to shove the ink about and something comes.

AUBREY VINCENT BEARDSLEY, *On Himself*

Grasp the subject, the words will follow.

MARCUS PORCIUS CATO, THE ELDER, *From Caius Julius Victor Ars Rhetorica*

How many good books suffer neglect through the inefficiency of their beginnings!

EDGAR ALLAN POE, *Marginalia*

Tom Birch is as brisk as a bee in conversation; but no sooner does he take a pen in his hand, than it becomes a torpedo to him, and benumbs all his faculties.

SAMUEL JOHNSON, Quoted in Boswell's *Life of Johnson*

'Where shall I begin, please your Majesty?' he asked.

'Begin at the beginning' the king said, gravely, 'and go on till you come to the end: then stop'.

LEWIS CARROLL, *Alice's Adventures in Wonderland*

Biting my truant pen, beating myself for spite: 'Fool!' said my Muse to me, 'look in thy heart and write'.

SIR PHILIP SIDNEY, *Astrophel and Stella*

Begin: to have commenced is half the deed. Half yet remains: begin again on this and thou wilt finish all.

DECIMUS MAGNUS AUSONIUS, *Epigrams*

## Thoughts and Thinking

There are a thousand thoughts lying within a man that he does not know till he takes up the pen to write.

WILLIAM MAKEPEACE THACKERAY, *Henry Esmond*

A single word even may be a spark of inextinguishable thought.

PERCY BYSSHE SHELLEY, *A Defence of Poetry*

Thinkers help other people to think, for they formulate what others are thinking. No person writes or thinks alone – thought is in the air, but its expression is necessary to create a tangible Spirit of the Times.

ELBERT HUBBARD, *Pig-Pen Pete*, 'The Bee'

Thoughts are but dreams till their effects be tried.

WILLIAM SHAKESPEARE, *The Rape of Lucrece*

He thought as a sage, though he felt as a man.

JAMES BEATTIE, *The Hermit*

A thought is often original, though you have uttered it a hundred times.

OLIVER WNEDELL HOLMES, *The Autocrat of the Breakfast Table*,
'Prologue'

Men grind and grind in the mill of a truism, and nothing comes out but what was put in. But the moment they desert the tradition for a spontaneous thought, then poetry, wit, hope, virtue, learning, anecdote, all flock to their aid.

RALPH WALDO EMERSON, *Literary Ethics*

There is not less wit nor invention in applying rightly a thought one finds in a book, than in being the first author of that thought.

PIERRE BAYLE, *Dictionnaire*

> *Lull'd in the countless chambers of the brain,*
> *Our thoughts are link'd by many a hidden chain;*
> *Awake but one, and lo, what myriads rise!*
> *Each stamps its image as the other flies.*
> ALEXANDER POPE, *An Essay on Criticism*

> *But far more numerous was the herd of such,*
> *Who think too little, and who talk too much.*
> JOHN DRYDEN, *Absalom and Achitophel*

One thought includes all thought, in the sense that a grain of sand includes the Universe.

SAMUEL TAYLOR COLERIDGE, *Additional Table Talk*, 'Thought'

The thoughts that come often unsought, and, as it were, drop into the mind, are commonly the most valuable of any we have.

JOHN LOCKE, *Letter to Samuel Bold*, 1699

> *Learning without thought is labour lost;*
> *thought without learning is perilous.*
> CONFUCIUS, *Analects*

A man is not idle because he is absorbed in thought. There is visible labour and there is an invisible labour.

VICTOR HUGO, *Les Misérables*

Thought makes every thing fit for use.

RALPH WALDO EMERSON, *Essays*, 'The Poet'

Thought is free.

WILLIAM SHAKESPEARE, *The Tempest*

*Such as take lodgings in a head*
*That's to be let unfurnished.*

SAMUEL BUTLER, *Hudibras*

When a thought takes one's breath away, a lesson on grammar seems an impertinence.

THOMAS WENTWORTH HIGGINSON,
*Preface to Emily Dickinson's Poems*

The very minute a thought is threatened with publicity it seems to shrink towards mediocrity.

OLIVER WENDELL HOLMES, *The Poet at the Breakfast Table*

When a thought is too weak to be expressed simply, it should be rejected.

MARQUIS DE LUC DE CLAPIERS VAUVENARGUES,
*Reflections and Maxims*

The highest possible stage in moral culture is when we recognize that we ought to control our thoughts.

CHARLES DARWIN, *The Descent of Man*

The mind ought sometimes to be amused, that it may the better return to thought, and to itself.

PHAEDRUS, *Fables*

This is a gift that I have, simple, simple; A foolish extravagant spirit, full of forms, figures, shapes, objects, ideas, apprehensions, motions, revolutions. These are begot in the ventricle of memory, nourished in the womb of pia mater; and delivered upon the mellowing of occasion. But the gift is good in those in whom it is acute, and I am thankful for it.

WILLIAM SHAKESPEARE, *Love's Labour's Lost*

*Oh! nature's noblest gift – my grey goose quill:*
*Slave of my thoughts, obedient to my will.*
*Torn from thy parent bird to form a pen.*
*That mighty instrument of little men!*
LORD BYRON, *English Bards and Scotch Reviewers*

They are never alone that are accompanied with noble thoughts.
SIR PHILIP SIDNEY, *Arcadia*

To think justly, we must understand what others mean: to know the value of our thoughts, we must try their effect on other minds.
WILLIAM HAZLITT, *The Plain Speaker*, 'On People of Sense'

The illusion that times that were are better than those that are, has probably pervaded all ages.
HORACE GREELEY, *The American Conflict*

How often misused words generate misleading thoughts.
HERBERT SPENCER, *Principles of Ethics*

*A boy's will is the wind's will,*
*And the thoughts of youth are long, long thoughts.*
HENRY WADSWORTH LONGFELLOW, *My Lost Youth*

Little minds are interested in the extraordinary; great minds in the commonplace.
ELBERT HUBBARD, *Roycroft Dictionary and Book of Epigrams*

No man ever forgot the visitations of that power to his heart and brain, which created all things new; which was the dawn in him of music, poetry, and art.
RALPH WALDO EMERSON, *Essays*, First Series, 'Love'

He thinks not well that thinks not again.
GEORGE HERBERT, *Jacula Prudentum*

*When any great design thou dost intend,*
*Think on the means, the manner, and the end.*
SIR JOHN DENHAM, *Of Prudence*

*I have no riches but my thoughts,*
*Yet these are wealth enough for me.*
SARA TEASDALE, *Love Songs*, 'Riches'

Literature is the Thought of thinking Souls.
THOMAS CARLYLE, *Essays*, 'Life of Scott'

The greatest thing a human soul ever does in this world is to see something. Hundreds of people can talk for one who thinks, but thousands can think for one who can see. To see clearly is poetry, prophecy and religion all in one.
JOHN RUSKIN, *Modern Painters*

I must have a prodigious quantity of mind; it takes me as much as a week, sometimes, to make it up.
MARK TWAIN, *The Innocents Abroad*

What is the hardest task in the world? To think.
RALPH WALDO EMERSON, *Essays*, First Series, 'Intellect'

To the vast majority of mankind nothing is more agreeable than to escape the need for mental exertion . . . To most people nothing is more troublesome than the effort of thinking.
JAMES BRYCE, *Studies in History and Jurisprudence*, 'Obedience'

There is no expedient to which man will not resort to avoid the real labour of thinking.
THOMAS ALVA EDISON, Placed on Signs around the
Edison laboratories, c.1895

We were to do more business after dinner; but after dinner is after dinner – An old saying and a tune, 'much drinking, little thinking.'
JONATHAN SWIFT, *Journal to Stella*

If a man sits down to think, he is immediately asked if he has the headache.
RALPH WALDO EMERSON, *Journals*, 1833

The mind of man is like a clock that is always running down and requires to be as constantly wound up.

WILLIAM HAZLITT, *Sketches and Essays*

Thinking means connecting things, and stops if they cannot be connected.

G. K. CHESTERTON, *Orthodoxy*

You may derive thoughts from others; Your way of thinking, the mould in which your thoughts are cast, must be your own.

CHARLES LAMB, *Essays of Elia*, 'The Old and the New
Schoolmaster'

A moment's thinking is an hour in words.

THOMAS HOOD, *Hero and Leander*

Man is obviously made to think. It is his whole dignity and his whole merit.

BLAISE PASCAL, *Pensées*

A mind quite vacant is a mind distressed.

WILLIAM COWPER, *Retirement*

Not pickt from the leaves of any author, but bred amongst the weeds and tares of mine own brain.

SIR THOMAS BROWNE, *Religio Medici*

A 'new thinker', when studied closely, is merely a man who does not know what other people have thought.

FRANK MOORE COLBY, *The Margin of Hesitation*

*We think so because other people think so,*
*Or because – or because – after all we do think so,*
*Or because we were told so, and think we must think so,*
*Or because we once thought so, and think we still think so,*
*Or because having thought so, we think we will think so.*

HENRY SIDGWICK, *Lines Composed in his Sleep*

## Ideas and Imagination

One of the greatest pains to human nature is the pain of a new idea.

WALTER BAGEHOT, *Physics and Politics*

That fellow seems to me to possess but one idea, and that is a wrong one.

SAMUEL JOHNSON, *Letter to Lord Chesterfield*, 1770

Nothing is more dangerous than an idea, when it is the only idea we have.

ALAIN (EMILE CHARTIER), *Libres-propos*

I maintain that ideas are events. It is more difficult to make them interesting I know, but if you fail the style is at fault.

GUSTAVE FLAUBERT, *Letter to Louise Colet*, 1853

All words are pegs to hang ideas on.

HENRY WARD BEECHER, *Proverbs from Plymouth Pulpit*, 'Human Mind'

For just when ideas fail, a word comes in to save the situation.

JOHANN WOLFGANG VON GOETHE, *Faust, Studierzimmer*

It is a lesson which all history teaches wise men, to put trust in ideas, and not in circumstances.

RALPH WALDO EMERSON, *Miscellanies*

The best ideas are common property.

SENECA, *Epistles*

Just as our eyes need light in order to see, our minds need ideas in order to conceive.

NICOLAS MALEBRANCHE, *Recherche de la vérité*

You can't depend on your judgment when your imagination is out of focus.

MARK TWAIN, *Note Book*

*The Possible's slow fuse is lit*
*By the Imagination.*

EMILY DICKINSON, *Poems*

He wants imagination, that's what he wants.

CHARLES DICKENS, *Barnaby Rudge*

One should operate by dissociation, and not by association, of ideas. An association is almost always commonplace. Dissociation decomposes, and uncovers latent affinities.

JULES RENARD, *Journal*, 1890

All great ideas are dangerous.

OSCAR WILDE, *De Profundis*

Any new formula which suddenly emerges in our consciousness has its roots in long trains of thought; it is virtually old when it first makes its appearance among the recognized growths of our intellect.

OLIVER WENDELL HOLMES, *The Autocrat of the Breakfast Table*

In mid-way flight imagination tires;
Yet soon re-prunes her wing to soar anew.

EDWARD YOUNG, *Night Thoughts*

There are no days in life so memorable as those which vibrated to some stroke of the imagination.

RALPH WALDO EMERSON, *Beauty, The Conduct of Life*

Imagination is as good as many voyages – and how much cheaper.

GEORGE WILLIAM CURTIS, *Prue and I*, Preface

Imagination is not a talent of some men but is the health of every man.

RALPH WALDO EMERSON, *Letters and Social Aims*,
'Poetry and Imagination'

## Knowledge and Experience

If a little knowledge is dangerous, where is the man who has so much as to be out of danger?

THOMAS HENRY HUXLEY, *Science and Culture*

Knowledge is proud that he has learned so much; Wisdom is humble that he knows no more.

WILLIAM COWPER, *The Task*, 'Winter Walk at Noon'

Knowledge is of two kinds. We know a subject ourselves, or we know where we can find information upon it.

SAMUEL JOHNSON, *Letter to William Strahan*, 1775

To be conscious that you are ignorant is a great step to knowledge.

BENJAMIN DISRAELI, *Sybil*

Knowledge is a treasure, but practice is the key to it.

THOMAS FULLER, *Gnomologia*

It is the peculiarity of knowledge that those who really thirst for it always get it.

RICHARD JEFFERIES, *Country Literature*

I find that I can have no enjoyment in the word but continual drinking of knowledge.

JOHN KEATS, *Letter to John Taylor*, 1818

I have taken all knowledge to be my province.

FRANCIS BACON, *Letter to Lord Burleigh*

An investment in knowledge pays the best interest.

BENJAMIN FRANKLIN, *Poor Richard*

Desire of knowledge, like the thirst for riches, increases ever with the acquisition of it.

LAURENCE STERNE, *Tristram Shandy*

The improvement of the understanding is for two ends: first, for our own increase of knowledge; secondly, to enable us to deliver and make out that knowledge to others.

JOHN LOCKE, *Some Thoughts Concerning Reading and Study*,
Appendix B

The knowledge of man is as the waters, some descending from above, and some springing up from beneath; the one informed by the light of nature, the other inspired by divine revelation.

FRANCIS BACON, *Advancement of Learning*

Knowledge must be adorned, it must have lustre as well as weight, or it will be oftener taken for lead than for gold.

LORD CHESTERFIELD, *Letters*, 1749

> *Wisdom is oftimes nearer when we stoop*
> *Than when we soar.*
> WILLIAM WORDSWORTH, *The Excursion*

In the world the important thing is not to know more than all men, but to know more at each moment than any particular man.

JOHANN WOLFGANG VON GOETHE, *Table Talk*

If you would know what nobody knows, read what everybody reads, just one year afterwards.

RALPH WALDO EMERSON, *Journals*, 1834

Knowledge and timber shouldn't be much used till they are seasoned.

OLIVER WENDELL HOLMES, *The Autocrat of the Breakfast Table*,
'The Chambered Nautilus'

Swallow all your learning in the morning, but digest it in company in the evenings.

LORD CHESTERFIELD, *Letters*, 1748

Common sense (which, in truth, is very uncommon) is the best sense
I know of.

LORD CHESTERFIELD, *Letters*, 1748

'Tis not knowing much, but what is useful, that makes a wise man.

THOMAS FULLER, *Gnomologia*

There is no subject so old that something new cannot be said about
it.

FYODOR MIKHAILOVICH DOSTOEVSKY, *A Diary of a Writer*, 1876

To know things well, we must know them in detail; but as that is
almost endless, our knowledge is always superficial and imperfect.

DUC DE LA ROCHEFOUCAULD, *Maxims*

> *All things I thought I knew; but now confess*
> *The more I know I know, I know the less.*
>
> ROBERT OWEN, *Works*, Bk. 6

All knowledge is of itself of some value. There is nothing so minute
or inconsiderable, that I would not rather know it than not.

SAMUEL JOHNSON, Quoted in Boswell's *Life of Johnson*

I honestly believe it iz better tew know nothing than tew know what
ain't so.

JOSH BILLINGS, *Encyclopedia of Proverbial Philosophy*

Since we cannot be universal and know all that is to be known of
everything, we ought to know a little about everything.

BLAISE PASCAL, *Pensées*

The reason why so few good books are written is that so few people
that can write know anything.

WALTER BAGEHOT, *Literary Studies*, 'Shakespeare'

What you don't know would make a great book.

SYDNEY SMITH, *Lady Holland, Memoir*

Culture is 'to know the best that has been said and thought in the world'.

MATTHEW ARNOLD, *Literature and Dogma*, Preface

Generalization is necessary to the advancement of knowledge; but particularity is indispensable to the creations of the imagination.

LORD MACAULAY, *Milton*

Knowledge is a comfortable and necessary retreat and shelter for us in an advanced age; and if we do not plant it while young, it will give us no shade when we grow old.

LORD CHESTERFIELD, *Letters to his son*, 1747

Make it thy business to know thyself, which is the most difficult lesson in the world.

MIGUEL DE CERVANTES, *Don Quixote*

We are wiser than we know.

RALPH WALDO EMERSON, *Essays*, First Series, 'The Over-Soul'

Exerience is the best of schoolmasters, only the school-fees are heavy.

THOMAS CARLYLE, *Miscellaneous Essays*

To most men, experience is like the stern lights of a ship, which illuminate only the track it has passed.

SAMUEL TAYLOR COLERIDGE, *Table Talk*

Young men's minds are always changeable, but when an old man is concerned in a matter, he looks both before and after.

HOMER, *The Iliad*

All experience is an arch, to build upon.

HENRY BROOKS ADAMS, *Education*

A moment's insight is sometimes worth a life's experience.

OLIVER WENDELL HOLMES, *The Professor at the Breakfast Table*

Many people know so little about what is beyond their short range of experience. They look within themselves – and find nothing! Therefore they conclude that there is nothing outside themselves, either.

HELEN KELLER, *The World I Live In*

> *By wisdom wealth is won;*
> *But riches purchased wisdom yet for none.*
> BAYARD TAYLOR, *The Wisdom of Ali*

> *When you find*
> *Bright passages that strike your mind.*
> *And which perhaps you may have reason*
> *To think on at another season, –*
> *Take them down in black and white.*
> JOHN BYROM, *Hint to a Young Person*

That's as well said, as if I had said it myself.

JONATHAN SWIFT, *Polite Conversation*

Experience is never limited, and it is never complete; it is an immense sensibility, a kind of huge spider-web of the finest silken threads suspended in the chamber of consciousness, and catching every air-borne particle in its tissue.

HENRY JAMES, *The Art of Fiction*, 'Partial Portraits'

The spectacles of experience; through them you will see clearly a second time.

HENRIK IBSEN, *The League of Youth*

Experience is the name everyone gives to his mistakes.

OSCAR WILDE, *Lady Windermere's Fan*

I have but one lamp by which my feet are guided, and that is the lamp of experience.

PATRICK HENRY, Speech, Virginia House of Delegates, 1775

# Style

When I read some of the rules for speaking and writing the English language correctly . . . I think –
> Any fool can make a rule
> And every fool will mind it.
HENRY DAVID THOREAU, *Journal*, 1860

Grammar is the grave of letters.
ELBERT HUBBARD, *A Thousand and One Epigrams*

This is the sort of English up with which I will not put.
SIR WINSTON CHURCHILL, Attributed. Marginal comment on document, on avoiding ending a sentence with a preposition – quoted by Sir Ernest Gowers in *Plain Words*

What is called style in writing or speaking is formed very early in life, while the imagination is warm and impressions are permanent.
THOMAS JEFFERSON, *Writings*

The most important things must be said simply, for they are spoiled by bombast; whereas trivial things must be described grandly, for they are supported only by aptness of expression, tone and manner.
JEAN DE LA BRUYÈRE, *Caractères*

Proper words in proper places, make the true definition of style.
JONATHAN SWIFT, *Letter to a Young Clergyman*, 1720

A strict and succinct style is that, where you can take away nothing without loss, and that loss be manifest.
BEN JONSON, *Explorata, Consuetudo*

The infallible test of a blameless style: namely, its untranslatableness in words of the same language, without injury to the meaning.
SAMUEL TAYLOR COLERIDGE, *Biographia Literaria*

When one finds a natural style, one is amazed and delighted, for

where one expected to see an author, one discovers a man.
BLAISE PASCAL, *Pensées*

A man knows what style of book he wants to write when he knows nothing else about it.
G. K. CHESTERTON, *Preface to Dickens's Pickwick Papers*

> Manner is all in all, whate'er is writ,
> The substitute for genius, sense, and wit.
> WILLIAM COWPER, *Table Talk*

## Wit

Among all kinds of writing, there is none in which authors are more apt to miscarry than in works of humour, as there is none in which they are more ambitious to excel.
JOSEPH ADDISON, *The Spectator*, No. 35

Don't put too fine a point to your wit, for fear it should get blunted.
MIGUEL DE CERVANTES, *Exemplary Novels, Little Gypsy*

Wit now and then, struck smartly, shows a spark.
WILLIAM COWPER, *Table Talk*

Their heads sometimes so little that there is no room for wit; sometimes so long that there is no wit for so much room.
THOMAS FULLER, *The Holy and the Profane State of Natural Fools*

The phrase 'unconscious humour' is the one contribution I have made to the current literature of the day.
SAMUEL BUTLER, *Note Books*

Men will confess to treason, murder, arson, false teeth, or a wig. How many of them will own up to a lack of humour?
FRANK MOORE COLBY, *The Colby Essays*, 'Satire and Teeth'

Wit makes its own welcome, and levels all distinctions. No dignity, no learning, no force of character, can make any stand against good wit.

RALPH WALDO EMERSON, *Letters and Social Aims*, 'The Comic'

> *Wit will shine*
> *Through the harsh cadence of a rugged line.*
> JOHN DRYDEN, *To the Memory of Mr Oldham*

No mind is thoroughly well organized that is deficient in a sense of humour.

SAMUEL TAYLOR COLERIDGE, *Table Talk*

I did not intend to write a funny book, at first. I did not know I was a humorist. I have never been sure about it.

JEROME K. JEROME, *My Life and Times*

> *And since, I never dare to write*
> *As funny as I can.*
> OLIVER WENDELL HOLMES, *The Height of the Ridiculous*

> *True wit is nature to advantage dress'd;*
> *What oft was thought, but ne'er so well express'd.*
> ALEXANDER POPE, *An Essay on Criticism*

Of all failures, to fail in a witticism is the worst, and the mishap is the more calamitous in a drawn out and detailed one.

WALTER SAVAGE LANDOR, *Imaginary Conversations*,
'Chesterfield and Chatham'

The humourist's like a man firin' at a target – he doesna ken whether he hits or no till them at the target tells 'im.

SIR JAMES MATTHEW BARRIE, *A Window in Thrums*

It is not enough to possess wit. One must have enough of it to avoid having too much.

ANDRÉ MAUROIS, *De la Conversation*

The wit we wish we had spoils the wit we have.
> JEAN BAPTISTE LOUIS GRESSET, *Le Méchant*

If you have wit, use it to please, and not to hurt: you may shine like the sun in the temperate zones, without scorching.
> LORD CHESTERFIELD, *Letters*, 1748

> *Endow me, if Thou grant me wit,*
> *Likewise with sense to mellow it.*
> DON MARQUIS, *Prayer*

There are several kinds of stories, but only one difficult kind – the humorous.
> MARK TWAIN, *How to Tell a Story*

Look, he's winding up the watch of his wit; by and by it will strike.
> WILLIAM SHAKESPEARE, *The Tempest*

The teller of a mirthful tale has latitude allowed him. We are content with less than absolute truth.
> CHARLES LAMB, *Last Essays of Elia*

> *You beat your pate, and fancy wit will come:*
> *Knock as you please, there's nobody at home.*
> ALEXANDER POPE, *Epigram*, 'An Empty House'

I can't say whether we had more wit amongst us now than usual, but I am certain we had more laughing, which answered the end as well.
> OLIVER GOLDSMITH, *The Vicar of Wakefield*

Laughter and tears are meant to turn the wheels of the same sensibility; one is wind-power and the other water-power, that is all.
> OLIVER WENDELL HOLMES, *The Autocrat of the Breakfast Table*

Surprise is so essential an ingredient of wit that no wit will bear repetition; – at least the original electrical feeling produced by any piece of wit can never be renewed.
> SYDNEY SMITH, *Lectures on Moral Philosophy*

*Some write, confin'd by physic; some, by debt;*
*Some, for 'tis Sunday; some, because 'tis wet; . . .*
*Another writes because his father writ,*
*And proves himself a bastard by his wit.*

EDWARD YOUNG, *Epistles to Mr Pope*

Many get the repute of being witty, but thereby lose the credit of being sensible. Jest has its little hour, seriousness should have all the rest.

BALTASAR GRACIÁN, *The Art of Worldly Wisdom*

*Nothing more smooth than glass, yet*
*nothing more brittle;*
*Nothing more fine than wit, yet*
*nothing more fickle.*

THOMAS FULLER, *Gnomologia*

Wit is the sudden marriage of ideas which before their union were not perceived to have any relation.

MARK TWAIN, *Notebook*

It is with wits as with razors, which are never so apt to cut those they are employed on as when they have lost their edge.

JONATHAN SWIFT, *Tale of a Tub*, Author's Preface

There is nothing breaks so many friendships as a difference of opinion as to what constitutes wit.

ELBERT HUBBARD, *Epigrams*

Oscar Wilde: I wish I had said that.
James McNeill Whistler: You will, Oscar, you will.

JAMES MCNEILL WHISTLER, Quoted in L. C. Ingleby,
*Oscar Wilde*

## Literature

To turn events into ideas is the function of literature.

GEORGE SANTAYANA, *Little Essays*

Literature is the art of writing something that will be read twice;
journalism what will be grasped at once.

CYRIL CONNOLLY, *Enemies of Promise*

Great Literature is simply language charged with meaning to the
utmost possible degree.

EZRA POUND, *How to Read*

There is first the literature of *knowledge*, and secondly, the literature
of *power*. The function of the first is – to *teach*; the function of the
second is – to *move*; the first is a rudder, the second an oar or a sail.
The first speaks to the *mere* discursive understanding; the second
speaks ultimately, it may happen, to the higher understanding of
reason.

THOMAS DE QUINCEY, *Essay on the Poets*, 'Pope'

Literature is not an abstract science, to which exact definitions can
be applied. It is an art, the success of which depends on personal
persuasiveness, on the author's skill to give as on ours to receive.

SIR ARTHUR QUILLER-COUCH, *Inaugural Lecture at
Cambridge University*, 1913

Writing is not literature unless it gives to the reader a pleasure which
arises not only from the things said, but from the way in which they
are said.

STOPFORD AUGUSTUS BROOKE, *Primer of English Literature*

In the civilization of today it is undeniable that, over all the arts,
literature dominates, serves beyond all.

WALT WHITMAN, *Democratic Vistas*

Literature exists to please – to lighten the burden of men's lives; to
make them for a short while forget their sorrows and their sins, their
silenced hearths, their disappointed hopes, their grim futures – and
those men of letters are the best loved who have best performed
literature's truest office.

AUGUSTINE BIRRELL, *Obiter Dicta*, 'Office of Literature'

Through all the works of Chaucer, there reigns a cheerfulness, a manly hilarity, which makes it almost impossible to doubt a correspondent habit of feeling in the author himself.

SAMUEL TAYLOR COLERIDGE, *Biographia Literaria*

Literature, like nobility, runs in the blood.

WILLIAM HAZLITT, *Table Talk*

It is life that shakes and rocks us; it is literature which stabilizes and confirms.

HEATHCOTE WILLIAM GARROD, *Profession of Poetry*

Literature was formerly an art and finance a trade: today it is the reverse.

JOSEPH ROUX, *Meditations of a Parish Priest*

Literature flourishes best when it is half a trade and half an art.

DEAN WILLIAM RALPH INGE, *The Victorian Age*

The literary world is made up of little confederacies, each looking upon its own members at the lights of the universe; and considering all others as mere transient meteors, doomed soon to fall and be forgotten, while its own luminaries are to shine steadily on to immortality.

WASHINGTON IRVING, *Literary Life*, 'Tales of a Traveller'

Literature in many of its branches is no other than the shadow of good talk.

ROBERT LOUIS STEVENSON, *Memories and Portraits*,
'Talk and Talkers'

No human being ever spoke of scenery for above two minutes at a time, which makes me suspect that we hear too much of it in literature.

ROBERT LOUIS STEVENSON, *Ibid.*

Literature does not please by moralizing us; it moralizes us because it pleases.

HEATHCOTE WILLIAM GARROD, *Profession of Poetry*

There is a great discovery still to be made in Literature, that of paying literary men by the quantity they do not write.

THOMAS CARLYLE, *Sir Walter Scott*

The land of literature is a fairy land to those who view it at a distance, but, like all other landscapes, the charm fades on a nearer approach, and the thorns and briars become visible. The republic of letters is the most factious and discordant of all republics, ancient or modern.

WASHINGTON IRVING, *Tales of a Traveller*, 'Notoriety'

Literature is an avenue to glory, ever open for those ingenious men who are deprived of honours or of wealth.

ISAAC D'ISRAELI, *Literary Character of Men of Genius*

Take the whole range of imaginative literature, and we are all wholesale borrowers. In every matter that relates to invention, to use, or beauty or form, we are borrowers.

WENDELL PHILLIPS, Lecture, *The Lost Arts*

To have lived in vain must be a painful thought to any man, and especially so to him who has made literature his profession.

SAMUEL TAYLOR COLERIDGE, *Biographia Literaria*

Literature – the most seductive, the most deceiving, the most dangerous of professions.

JOHN, VISCOUNT MORLEY, *Critical Miscellanies*, 'Burke'

## History and Biography

It takes a great deal of history to produce a little literature.

HENRY JAMES, *Life of Nathaniel Hawthorne*

The only lesson history has taught us is that man has not yet learned anything from history.

ANON

History is only a confused heap of facts.

LORD CHESTERFIELD, *Letter to his son*, 1750

Living in the past has one thing in its favour – it's cheaper.

ANON

Historians relate, not so much what is done, as what they would have believed.

BENJAMIN FRANKLIN, *Poor Richard*

The historian must not try to know what is truth, if he values his honesty; for, if he cares for his truths, he is certain to falsify his facts.

HENRY ADAMS, *The Education of Henry Adams*

I often wish that I could rid the world of the tyranny of facts. What are facts but compromises? A fact merely marks the point where we have agreed to let investigation cease.

BLISS CARMAN, In the *Atlantic Monthly*, 1906

The philosophy of one century is the common sense of the next.

HENRY WARD BEECHER, *Life Thoughts*

Wherever men have lived there is a story to be told, and it depends chiefly on the story-teller or historian whether that is interesting or not.

HENRY DAVID THOREAU, *Journal*, 1860

More difficult to do a thing than to talk about it? Not at all. That is a gross popular error. It is very much more difficult to talk about a thing than to do it. In the sphere of actual life that is of course obvious. Anyone can make history. Only a great man can write it.

OSCAR WILDE, *The Critic as Artist*

History is the essence of innumerable biographies.

THOMAS CARLYLE, *Essay on History*

Biography is by nature the most universally profitable, universally pleasant of all things: especially biography of distinguished individuals.

THOMAS CARLYLE, *Sartor Resartus*, Bk. I

How inexpressibly comfortable to know our fellow-creature; to see into him, understand his goings-forth, decipher the whole heart of his mystery: nay, not only to see into him, but even to see out of him, to view the world altogether as he views it.

THOMAS CARLYLE, *Biography*

The first thing to be done by a biographer in estimating character is to examine the stubs of the victim's cheque-books.

SILAS WEIR MITCHELL, Quoted in Cushing, *Life of Sir William Osler*

## Novels

When writing a novel a writer should create living people; people not characters. A *character* is a caricature.

ERNEST HEMINGWAY, *Death in the Afternoon*

A novel is a mirror walking along a main road.

STENDHAL (HENRI BEYLE), *Le Rouge et le Noir*

A good novel tells us the truth about its hero; but a bad novel tells us the truth about its author.

G. K. CHESTERTON, *Heretics*

Novelists should never allow themselves to weary of the study of real life.

CHARLOTTE BRONTË, *The Professor*

The only reason for the existence of a novel is that it does attempt to represent life.

HENRY JAMES, *The Art of Fiction*

Fiction is like a spider's web, attached ever so slightly perhaps, but still attached to life at all four corners.

VIRGINIA WOOLF, *A Room of One's Own*

Plots are no more exhausted than men are. Every man is a new creation, and combinations are simply endless.

CHARLES DUDLEY WARNER, *Backlog Studies, Sixth Study*

Make 'em laugh; make 'em cry; make 'em wait.

CHARLES READE, *Recipe for a Successful Novel*

> 'Tis strange – but true; for truth is always strange;
> Stranger than fiction: if it could be told,
> How much would novels gain by the exchange.

LORD BYRON, *Don Juan*

Fiction carries a greater amount of truth in solution than the volume which purports to be all true.

WILLIAM MAKEPEACE THACKERAY, *The English Humorists*,
'Steele'

History is a novel which did take place; a novel is history that could take place.

EDMOND AND JULES DE GONCOURT, *Idées et sensations*

The ancient historians gave us delightful fiction in the form of fact; the modern novelist presents us with dull facts under the guise of fiction.

OSCAR WILDE, *The Decay of Lying*

What is a novel if not a conviction of our fellow-men's existence strong enough to take upon itself a form of imagined life clearer than reality and whose accumulated verisimilitude of selected episodes puts to shame the pride of documentary history?

JOSEPH CONRAD, *A Personal Record*

Great is the poverty of novelists' inventions. She was beautiful and he fell in love.

RALPH WALDO EMERSON, *Society and Solitude*, 'Books'

The good ended happily, the bad unhappily. That is what fiction means.

OSCAR WILDE, *The Importance of Being Earnest*

'And what are you reading, Miss – ?'
'Oh! it is only a novel!' replies the young lady: while she lays down her book with affected indifference, or momentary shame.
– 'It is only Cecilia, or Camilla, or Belinda:' or, in short, only some work in which the most thorough knowledge of human nature, the happiest delineation of its varieties, the liveliest effusions of wit and humour are conveyed to the world in the best chosen language.

JANE AUSTEN, *Northanger Abbey*

When I want to read a novel I write one.

BENJAMIN DISRAELI, *Attributed*

He always hurries into the midst of the story as if they knew it already.

HORACE, *Ars Poetica*

From a mere nothing springs a mighty tale.

PROPERTIUS, *Elegies*

With a tale forsooth he cometh unto you, with a tale which holdeth children from play, and old men from the chimney corner.

SIR PHILIP SIDNEY, *The Defence of Poesy*

Not that the story need be long, but it will take a long while to make it short.

HENRY DAVID THOREAU, *Letter*, 1857

Persons attempting to find a motive in this narrative will be prosecuted; persons attempting to find a moral in it will be banished; persons attempting to find a plot in it will be shot.

MARK TWAIN, *The Adventures of Huckleberry Finn*

Walter Scott has no business to write novels, especially good ones. It is not fair. He has Fame and Profit enough as a Poet, and should not be taking the bread out of other people's mouths.

I do not like him, and do not mean to like *Waverley* if I can help it . . . but fear I must.

JANE AUSTEN, *Letter to Anna Austen*, 1814

# 5
# Talent and Genius

If you have great talents, industry will improve them: if you have but moderate abilities, industry will supply their deficiency.

SIR JOSHUA REYNOLDS, *Discourses*

> *Hide not your talents, they for use were made.*
> *What's a Sun-Dial in the Shade?*
>
> BENJAMIN FRANKLIN, *Poor Richard*

All our talents increase in the using, and every faculty, both good and bad, strengthens by exercise.

ANNE BRONTË, *The Tenant of Wildfell Hall*

Talent alone cannot make a writer. There must be a man behind the book.

RALPH WALDO EMERSON, *Representative Men*, Goethe, 1850

Talent is formed in quiet; character in the stream of human life.

JOHANN WOLFGANG VON GOETHE, *Tasso*

Talent is a question of quantity. Talent does not write one page: it writes three hundred.

JULES RENARD, *Journal*, 1887

To do easily what others find difficult is talent; doing what is impossible *for talent* is genius.

HENRI-FRÉDÉRIC AMIEL, *Journal*, 1856

The world is always ready to receive talent with open arms. Very

often it does not know what to do with genius.
OLIVER WENDELL HOLMES, *The Professor at the Breakfast Table*

Talent, lying in the understanding, is often inherited; genius, being the action of reason and imagination, rarely or never.
SAMUEL TAYLOR COLERIDGE, *Table Talk*

There is the same difference between talent and genius that there is between a stone mason and a sculptor.
ROBERT GREEN INGERSOLL, *Shakespeare*

Genius is one per cent inspiration and ninety-nine per cent perspiration.
THOMAS ALVA EDISON, *Life*

Genius is only a greater aptitude for patience.
COMTE DE BUFFON, Attributed

Genius . . . has been defined as a supreme capacity for taking trouble . . .
It might be more fitly described as a supreme capacity for getting its possessors into trouble of all kinds and keeping them therein so long as the genius remains.
SAMUEL BUTLER, *Genius*

Two sorts of writers possess genius: those who think, and those who cause others to think.
JOSEPH ROUX, *Meditations of a Parish Priest*,
'Literature: Poets'

Good God! what a genius I had when I wrote that book.
JONATHAN SWIFT, *A Tale of a Tub*

I have nothing to declare except my genius.
OSCAR WILDE, At New York Custom House

Great geniuses have the shortest biographies.
RALPH WALDO EMERSON, *Representative Men*, 'Plato'

Genius, in one respect, is like gold, – numbers of persons are constantly writing about *both*, who have *neither*.

CHARLES CALEB COLTON, *Lacon*

Everyone is a genius at least once a year. The real geniuses simply have their bright ideas closer together.

GEORG CHRISTOPH LICHTENBERG, *Aphorisms*

There is no work of genius which has not been the delight of mankind, no word of genius to which the human heart and soul have not, sooner or later, responded.

JAMES RUSSELL LOWELL, *Among My Books*,
'Rousseau and the Sentimentalists'

The definition of genius is that it acts unconsciously; and those who have produced immortal works have done so without knowing how or why.

WILLIAM HAZLITT, *The Plain Speaker*, 'Whether genius is
conscious of its powers.'

Men of Genius are often dull and inert in society, as the blazing meteor when it descends to the earth is only a stone.

HENRY WADSWORTH LONGFELLOW, *Kavanagh*

> *Genius, that power which dazzles mortal eyes,*
> *Is oft but perseverance in disguise.*

HENRY WILLARD AUSTIN, *Perseverance Conquers All*

Genius seems to consist merely in trueness of sight, in using such words as show that the man was an eye-witness, and not a repeater of what was told.

RALPH WALDO EMERSON, *Journals*, 1834

Perhaps, moreover, he whose genius appears deepest and truest excels his fellows in nothing save the knack of expression; he throws out occasionally a lucky hint at truths of which every human soul is profoundly though unutterably conscious.

> NATHANIEL HAWTHORNE, *The Procession of Life*,
> 'Mosses from an Old Manse'

Towering genius disdains a beaten path. It seeks regions hitherto unexplored.

> ABRAHAM LINCOLN, Address at the Young Men's Lyceum,
> Springfield, Illinois, 1838

The public is wonderfully tolerant. It forgives everything except genius.

> OSCAR WILDE, *The Critic as Artist*, 'Intentions'

Genius always finds itself a century too early.

> RALPH WALDO EMERSON, *Journals*, 1840

In every work of genius we recognize our own rejected thoughts: they come back to us with a certain alienated majesty.

> RALPH WALDO EMERSON, *Essays*, First Series, 'Self-Reliance'

No author is a man of genius to his publisher.

> HEINRICH HEINE, *Works*

Unless one is a genius, it is best to aim at being intelligible.

> ANTHONY HOPE, *The Dolly Dialogues*

## Success and Fame

The only person who thought writing was easy was writing the word *backwards* . . . forwards at the time.

> ANON

The secret of success in life is known only to those who have not succeeded.

> JOHN CHURTON COLLINS, *Aphorisms*

The line between failure and success is so fine that we scarcely know when we pass it: so fine that we are often on the line and do not know it.

ELBERT HUBBARD, _The Note Book_

Nothing is more humiliating than to see idiots succeed in enterprises we have failed in.

GUSTAVE FLAUBERT, _Sentimental Education_

The ability to convert ideas to things is the secret of outward success.

HENRY WARD BEECHER, _Proverbs from Plymouth Pulpit_

We learn wisdom from failure much more than from success. We often discover what _will_ do, by finding out what will not do; and probably he who never made a mistake never made a discovery.

SAMUEL SMILES, _Self-Help_

The way to secure success is to be more anxious about obtaining than about deserving it.

WILLIAM HAZLITT, 'On the Qualifications Necessary to Success in Life', _The Plain Speaker_

The best preparation for good work tomorrow is to do good work today.

ELBERT HUBBARD, _The Note Book_

In order that people may be happy in their work, these three things are needed: They must be fit for it. They must not do too much of it. And they must have a sense of success in it.

JOHN RUSKIN, _Pre-Raphaelitism_

A successful man cannot realize how hard an unsuccessful man finds life.

EDGAR WATSON HOWE, _Country Town Sayings_

The Dictionary is available to every writer. All they need, thereafter, is to select the right words from within it and string them together in the right order, like the coloured beads of a necklace, to achieve success, fame and even fortune.

ANON

Some men succeed by what they know; some by what they do; and a few by what they are.

ELBERT HUBBARD, *The Note Book*

We never do anything well till we cease to think about the manner of doing it.

WILLIAM HAZLITT, *Sketches and Essays*, 'On Prejudice'

The success of most things depends upon knowing how long it will take to succeed.

MONTESQUIEU, *Pensées diverses*

Constant success shows us but one side of the world. For as it surrounds us with friends who will tell us only our merits, so it silences those enemies from whom alone we can learn our defects.

CHARLES CALEB COLTON, *Lacon*

The reward of a thing well done is to have done it.

RALPH WALDO EMERSON, *Essays*, 'New England Reformers'

To succeed in the world, we do everything we can to appear successful.

DUC DE LA ROCHEFOUCAULD, *Reflections*

A minute's success pays the failure of years.

ROBERT BROWNING, *Apollo and the Fates*

> *Success is counted sweetest*
> *By those who ne'er succeed.*

EMILY DICKINSON, *Poems*

Pray that success will not come any faster than you are able to endure it.

ELBERT HUBBARD, *The Note Book*

Success is not greedy, as people think, but insignificant. That's why it satisfies nobody.

LUCIUS ANNAEUS SENECA, *Letters to Lucilius*

I look on that man as happy, who, when there is question of success, looks into his work for a reply.

RALPH WALDO EMERSON, *Conduct of Life*, 'Worship'

Literary fame is the only fame of which a wise man ought to be ambitious, because it is the only lasting and living fame.

ROBERT SOUTHEY, Quoted in Forster's *Life of Landor*

Every great and original writer, in proportion as he is great and original, must himself create the taste by which he is to be relished.

WILLIAM WORDSWORTH, *Letter to Lady Beaumont*,
21 May, 1807

I would sooner fail than not be among the greatest.

JOHN KEATS, *Letter to J. A. Hessey*, 1818

Fame is delightful, but as collateral it does not rank high.

ELBERT HUBBARD, *Epigrams*

He that cometh in print because he would be known, is like the fool that cometh into the Market because he would be seen.

JOHN LYLY, *Euphues*, 'To the Gentlemen Readers'

Nothing is so commonplace as to wish to be remarkable.

OLIVER WENDELL HOLMES, *The Autocrat of the Breakfast Table*

Fame sometimes hath created something of nothing.

THOMAS FULLER, *The Holy and the Profane State*, 'Fame'

Men have a solicitude about fame; and the greater share they have of it, the more afraid they are of losing it.

SAMUEL JOHNSON, Quoted in Boswell's *Life of Johnson*

Fame has also this great drawback, that if we pursue it we must

direct our lives in such a way as to please the fancy of men, avoiding what they dislike and seeking what is pleasing to them.
BARUCH SPINOZA, *On the Correction of the Understanding*

No man was ever great without some portion of divine inspiration.
MARCUS TULLIUS CICERO, *De Natura Deorum*

Some men are born great, some achieve greatness, and some have greatness thrust upon them.
WILLIAM SHAKESPEARE, *Twelfth Night*

The talent of success is nothing more than doing what you can do well; and doing well whatever you do, without a thought of fame.
HENRY WADSWORTH LONGFELLOW, *Hyperion*

I awoke one morning and found myself famous.
LORD BYRON, Entry in Memoranda after publication of
*Childe Harold*

Fame, we may understand, is no sure test of merit, but only a probability of such: it is an accident, not a property of a Man.
THOMAS CARLYLE, *Essays*, 'Goethe'

*Some for renown, on scraps of learning dote,*
*And think they grow immortal as they quote.*
EDWARD YOUNG, *Love of Fame*

*Lives of great men all remind us*
*We can make our lives sublime,*
*And, departing, leave behind us*
*Footprints on the sands of time.*
HENRY WADSWORTH LONGFELLOW, *A Psalm of Life*

It took me fifteen years to discover I had no talent for writing, but I couldn't give it up because by that time I was too famous.
ROBERT BENCHLEY, *On Himself*

> *In short, whoever you may be,*
> *To this conclusion you'll agree,*
> *When everyone is somebodee,*
> *Then no one's anybody!*
> SIR WILLIAM SCHWENK GILBERT, *The Gondoliers*

While we are asleep, we are all equal.

> MIGUEL DE CERVANTES, *Don Quixote*

# 6
# Titles

Were it inquired of an ingenious writer what page of his work had occasioned his most perplexity, he would often point to the title-page. The curiosity which we there would excite is, however, most fastidious to gratify.

ISAAC D'ISRAELI, *Curiosities of Literature*

*The Ancient Mariner* would not have taken so well if it had been called *The Old Sailor*.

SAMUEL BUTLER, *Note-Books*, 'Titles and Subjects'

Suit your Title to your Book; and through past centuries take a look. For wherever there are quotations, titles abound.

ANON

> *I would not enter on my list of friends*
> *(Though graced with polished manners and fine sense,*
> *Yet wanting sensibility) the man*
> *Who needlessly sets foot upon a worm.*

WILLIAM COWPER, *The Task*, 'The Winter Walk at Noon'

(*Sense and Sensibility* – title of the novel by Jane Austen)

'The whole of this unfortunate business,' said Dr Lyster, 'has been the result of Pride and Prejudice.'

FANNY BURNEY, *Cecilia*

(*Pride and Prejudice* – title of the novel by Jane Austen)

> *Far from the madding crowd's ignoble strife*
> *Their sober wishes never learn'd to stray;*

*Along the cool sequester'd vale of life*
*They kept the noiseless tenor of their way.*
        THOMAS GRAY, *Elegy in a Country Churchyard*

(*Far From The Madding Crowd* – title of the novel by Thomas Hardy)

*Fame is the spur that the clear spirit doth raise*
*(That last infirmity of noble mind)*
*To scorn delights, and live laborious days.*
        JOHN MILTON, *Lycidas*

(*Fame is the Spur* – title of the novel by Howard Spring)

. . . any man's death diminishes me, because I am involved in mankind; and therefore never send to know for whom the bell tolls; it tolls for thee.
        JOHN DONNE, *Devotions*

(*For Whom The Bell Tolls* – title of the novel by *Ernest Hemingway*)

The last enemy that shall be destroyed is death.
        I CORINTHIANS

(*The Last Enemy* – title of the book written by Richard Hillary, RAF fighter-pilot, just before he was killed in action during World War 2)

*Fair stood the wind for France*
*When we our sails advance,*
*Nor now to prove our chance*
*Longer will tarry.*
        MICHAEL DRAYTON, *The Ballad of Agincourt*

(*Fair Stood The Wind For France* – title of the novel by H. E. Bates)

*Shall I compare thee to a summer's day?*
*Thou art more lovely and more temperate:*
*Rough winds do shake the darling buds of May,*
*And summer's lease hath all too short a date.*
*But thy eternal summer shall not fade.*
        WILLIAM SHAKESPEARE, *Sonnets*

(*The Darling Buds Of May* – title of the novel by H. E. Bates)

More (Sir Thomas More) is a man . . . (ends) . . . a man for all seasons.

ROBERT WHITTINGTON, Passage composed c.1521
for schoolboys to put into Latin

(*A Man For All Seasons* – title of the play written by Robert Bolt, and subsequently a screenplay)

> *I must go down to the seas again, to the*
> *lonely sea and the sky,*
> *And all I ask is a tall ship and a star to*
> *steer her by . . .*

JOHN MASEFIELD, *Sea Fever*

(*The Lonely Sea and the Sky* – autobiography of Francis Chichester, pioneer navigator, yachtsman, and pilot. Knighted by Queen Elizabeth II after sailing alone around the world in Gipsy Moth IV, 1967)

> *He prayeth well, who loveth well*
> *Both man and bird and beast.*
> *He prayeth best, who loveth best*
> *All things both great and small;*
> *For the dear God who loveth us,*
> *He made and loveth all.*

SAMUEL TAYLOR COLERIDGE, *The Ancient Mariner*

> *All things bright and beautiful,*
> *All creatures great and small,*
> *All things wise and wonderful,*
> *The Lord God made them all.*

CECIL FRANCES ALEXANDER, *All Things Bright and Beautiful*

(*All Creatures Great and Small, All Things Bright and Beautiful, All Things Wise and Wonderful, The Lord God Made Them All* – titles of books written by *James Herriot*)

# 7
# Poets

The art of the pen is to rouse the inward vision . . . That is why the poets, who spring imagination with a word or a phrase, paint lasting pictures.

GEORGE MEREDITH, *Diana of the Crossways*

> *There is a pleasure in poetic pains*
> *Which only poets know.*
> WILLIAM COWPER, *The Task*, 'The Timepiece'

No man was ever yet a great poet, without being at the same time a profound philosopher.

SAMUEL TAYLOR COLERIDGE, *Biographia Literaria*

For a good poet's made as well as born.

BEN JONSON, *To the Memory of Shakespeare*

> *The poet's eye, in a fine frenzy rolling,*
> *Doth glance from heaven to earth, from earth to heaven;*
> *And, as imagination bodies forth*
> *The forms of things unknown, the poet's pen*
> *Turns them to shapes, and gives to airy nothing*
> *A local habitation and a name.*
> WILLIAM SHAKESPEARE, *A Midsummer Night's Dream*

All great epic poets compose their fine poems not from art, but because they are inspired and possessed.

PLATO, *Ion*

*And they shall be accounted poet kings*
*Who simply tell the most heart-easing things.*

JOHN KEATS, *Sleep and Poetry*

To a poet nothing can be useless.

SAMUEL JOHNSON, *Rasselas*

All men are poets at heart.

RALPH WALDO EMERSON, *Nature, Addresses, and Lectures,*
'Literary Ethics'

I wish our clever young poets would remember my homely definitions of prose and poetry; that is, prose = words in their best order; poetry = the *best* words in the best order.

SAMUEL TAYLOR COLERIDGE, *Table Talk*

To poets to be second-rate is a privilege which neither men, nor gods, nor bookstalls ever allowed.

HORACE, *Ars Poetica*

Whatever a poet writes with enthusiasm and a divine inspiration is very fine.

DEMOCRITUS, *Fragment*

If the works of the great poets teach anything, it is to hold mere invention somewhat cheap. It is not the finding of a thing, but the making something out of it after it is found, that is of consequence.

JAMES RUSSELL LOWELL, *My Study Windows*, 'Chaucer'

Nature herself seems, I say, to take the pen out of his [Wordsworth's] hand, and to write for him with her own bare, sheer, penetrating power.

MATTHEW ARNOLD, *Preface to Poems of Wordsworth*

The majority of poems one outgrows and outlives, as one outgrows and outlives the majority of human passions. Dante's is one of those that one can only just hope to grow up to at the end of life.

T. S. ELIOT, *Selected Essays*, 'Dante'

You would think it strange if I called Burns the most gifted British soul we had in all that century of his: and yet I believe the day is coming when there will be little danger in saying so.

THOMAS CARLYLE, *On Heroes and Hero-Worship*,
'On Robert Burns'

Byron wrote, as easily as a hawk flies, and as clearly as a lake reflects, the exact truth in the precisely narrowest terms.

JOHN RUSKIN, *Praeterita*, 'On Lord Byron'

*No slightest golden rhyme he wrote*
*That held not something men must quote;*
*Thus by design or chance did he*
*Drop anchors to posterity.*

THOMAS BAILEY ALDRICH, *A Hint from Herrick*

Coleridge was the first poet I ever knew. He talked on for ever; and you wished him to talk on for ever. His thoughts did not seem to come with labour and effort; but as if borne on the gusts of genius, and as if the wings of his imagination lifted him from off his feet. His mind was clothed with wings; and raised on them, he lifted philosophy to heaven.

WILLIAM HAZLITT, *Lectures on the English Poets*,
'Samuel Taylor Coleridge'

The sympathy of the poet with the subjects of his poetry is particularly remarkable in Shakespeare and Chaucer; but what the first effects by a strong act of imagination and mental metamorphosis, the last does without any effort, merely by the inborn kindly joyousness of his nature. How well we seem to know Chaucer! How absolutely nothing do we know of Shakespeare.

SAMUEL TAYLOR COLERIDGE, *Table Talk*

He (Shakespeare) was not of an age, but for all time!

BEN JONSON, *To the Memory of My Beloved,*
*the Author, Mr William Shakespeare*

John Dryden was certainly a mechanical maker of verses, and in every line he ever wrote, we see indubitable marks of the most indefatigable industry and labour.

WILLIAM COWPER, *Letter to Unwin*

John Dryden has often said to me in confidence, that the world would have never suspected him to be so great a poet, if he had not assured them so frequently in his prefaces that it was impossible they could either doubt or forget it.

JONATHAN SWIFT, *A Tale of a Tub*

Those miserable mountebanks of the day, the poets, disgrace themselves and deny God, in running down Pope, the most *faultless* of Poets, and almost of men.

LORD BYRON, Writing of Alexander Pope in
*Letter to John Murray*, 1820

It is surely superfluous to answer the question that has once been asked, Whether Pope was a poet? otherwise than by asking in return, If Pope be not a poet, where is poetry to be found?

SAMUEL JOHNSON, *Lives of the English Poets*

It might be fairly urged that I have less poetical sentiment than Tennyson, and less intellectual vigour and abundance than Browning; yet, because I have perhaps more of a fusion of the two than either of them . . . I am likely enough to have my turn, as they have had theirs.

MATTHEW ARNOLD, *Letter to his Mother*, 1869

The works of the great poets have never yet been read by mankind, for only great poets can read them.

HENRY DAVID THOREAU, *Walden, Reading*

Next to being a great poet, is the power of understanding one.

HENRY WADSWORTH LONGFELLOW, *Hyperion*, Bk. 2

All that is best in the great poets of all countries is not what is national in them, but what is universal.

HENRY WADSWORTH LONGFELLOW, *Kavanagh*

All great poets have been men of great knowledge.
> WILLIAM CULLEN BRYANT, *Lectures on Poetry*,
> 'Relation of Poetry to Time and Place'

Nine-tenths of the best poetry of the world has been written by poets less than thirty years old; a great deal more than half of it has been written by poets under twenty-five.
> HENRY LOUIS MENCKEN, *Prejudices*

There was never poet who had not the heart in the right place.
> RALPH WALDO EMERSON, *Society and Solitude*, 'Success'

It is a man's sincerity and depth of vision that makes him a poet.
> THOMAS CARLYLE, *On Heroes and Hero-Worship*

Do not judge the poet's life to be sad because of his plaintive verses and confessions of despair. Because he was able to cast off his sorrows into these writings, therefore went he onward free and serene to new experiences.
> RALPH WALDO EMERSON, *Journals*

I do distrust the poet who discerns no character or glory in his times.
> ELIZABETH BARRETT BROWNING, *Aurora Leigh*

> *Most joyful let the Poet be;*
> *It is through him that all men see.*
> WILLIAM ELLERY CHANNING, *The Poet of the Old*
> *and New Times*

The experience of each new age requires a new confession, and the world seems always waiting for its poet.
> RALPH WALDO EMERSON, *Essays*, Second Series, 'The Poet'

> *All the poet can do today is to warn.*
> *That is why the true Poets must be truthful.*
> WILFRED OWEN, *Poems*

The truth, which is a standard for the naturalist, for the poet is only a stimulus.

GEORGE SANTAYANA, *Soliloquies in England*, 'Ideas'

The sign and credentials of the poet are that he announces that which no man has foretold.

RALPH WALDO EMERSON, *Essays*, Second Series, 'The Poet'

The proof of a poet is that his country absorbs him as affectionately as he has absorbed it.

WALT WHITMAN, Preface to *Leaves of Grass*

To have great poets, there must be great audiences, too.

WALT WHITMAN, *Notes Left Over*: 'Ventures,
on an Old Theme'

To know how to say what other people only think, is what makes men poets and sages.

ELIZABETH RUNDLE CHARLES, *Chronicles of the
Schönberg-Cotta Family*

The business of a poet, said Imlac, is to examine, not the individual, but the species; to remark general properties and large appearances: he does not number the streaks of the tulip, or describe the different shades in the verdure of the forest.

SAMUEL JOHNSON, *Rasselas*

> '*Give me a theme*,' the little poet cried,
> '*And I will do my part*,'
> "*Tis not a theme you need*,' the world replied;
> '*You need a heart*.'

RICHARD WATSON GILDER, *Wanted, a Theme*

We can say nothing but what hath been said . . . Our poets steal from Homer . . . He that comes last is commonly best.

ROBERT BURTON, *Anatomy of Melancholy*,
'Democritus to the Reader'

Subtract from many modern poets all that may be found in Shakespeare, and trash will remain.

CHARLES CALEB COLTON, *Lacon*

> *So, naturalists observe, a flea*
> *Hath smaller fleas that on him prey;*
> *And these have smaller fleas to bite 'em,*
> *And so proceed* ad infinitum.
> *Thus every poet, in his kind,*
> *Is bit by him that comes behind.*

JONATHAN SWIFT, *On Poetry*

The little girl had the making of a poet in her who, being told to be sure of her meaning before she spoke, said: 'How can I know what I think till I see what I say?'

GRAHAM WALLAS, *The Art of Thought*

Knowledge of the subject is to the poet what durable materials are to the architect.

SAMUEL JOHNSON, *Works*

Poets are the only poor fellows in the world whom anybody will flatter.

ALEXANDER POPE, *Letter to Wm. Trumbull*, 1713

Modesty is a virtue not often found among poets; for almost every one of them thinks himself the greatest in the world.

MIGUEL DE CERVANTES, *Don Quixote*

All poets pretend to write for immortality, but the whole tribe have no objection to present pay and present praise.

CHARLES CALEB COLTON, *Lacon*

> *Oh! many are the Poets that are sown*
> *By Nature; men endowed with highest gifts,*
> *The vision and the faculty divine;*
> *Yet wanting the accomplishment of verse.*

WILLIAM WORDSWORTH, *The Excursion*

According to that old verse . . . Astronomers, painters and poets may lie by authority.

SIR JOHN HARINGTON, *Apologie of Poetry*

> *When people say, 'I've told you* fifty *times,'*
> *They mean to scold, and very often do;*
> *When poets say, 'I've written* fifty *rhymes,'*
> *They make you dread that they'll recite them too.*
>
> LORD BYRON, *Don Juan*

Poets ever fail in reading their own verses to their worth.

ELIZABETH BARRETT BROWNING, *Lady Geraldine's Courtship*

Poets have often nothing poetical about them except their verses.

RALPH WALDO EMERSON, *Conduct of Life*, 'Behaviour'

My father discouraged me by ridiculing my performances, and telling me verse-makers were generally beggars.

BENJAMIN FRANKLIN, *Autobiography*

> *Poets, being poor,*
> *Must use words with economy.*
>
> WILLIAM GRIFFITH, *Laconic*

> *Poets, henceforth for pensions need not care,*
> *Who call you beggars, you may call them liars,*
> *Verses are grown such merchantable ware,*
> *That now for Sonnets, sellers are, and buyers.*
>
> SIR JOHN HARINGTON, *Epigrams*, 'A Comfort for Poor Poets'

A poet can survive everything but a misprint.

OSCAR WILDE, *The Children of the Poets*

Let such as have not got a passport from nature be content with happiness, and leave to the poet the unrivalled possession of his misery, his garret, and his fame.

OLIVER GOLDSMITH, *The Poet*, Critical Review, 1759

It is a better and a wiser thing to be a starved apothecary than a starved poet; so back to the shop Mr John, back to 'plasters, pills, and ointment boxes'.

> JOHN GIBSON LOCKHART, Review of Keats' *Endymion* in
> *Blackwood's Magazine*

> *It is not poetry that makes men poor,*
> *For few do write that were not so before,*
> *And those that have writ best, had they been rich,*
> *Had ne'er been clapp'd with a poetic itch.*
> SAMUEL BUTLER, *Miscellaneous Thoughts*

Could a man live by it, it were not unpleasant employment to be a poet.

> OLIVER GOLDSMITH, *Letter to H. Goldsmith*

# 8
# Poetry

Good poetry could not have been otherwise written than it is. The first time you hear it, it sounds rather as if copied out of some invisible tablet in the Eternal mind, than as if arbitrarily composed by the poet. The feeling of all great poets has accorded with this. They found the verse, not made it. The muse brought it to them.

RALPH WALDO EMERSON, *Essays*, First Series, '*Art*'

Poetry lifts the veil from the hidden beauty of the world, and makes familiar objects be as if they were not familiar.

PERCY BYSSHE SHELLEY, *A Defence of Poetry*

What is poetry? The suggestion, by the imagination, of noble grounds for the noble emotions.

JOHN RUSKIN, *Modern Painters*, 1888

Poetry is simply the most beautiful, impressive, and widely effective mode of saying things, and hence its importance.

MATTHEW ARNOLD, *Essays in Criticism*, 'Functions of Criticism at the Present Time. Heinrich Heine'

Music is the universal language of mankind – poetry their universal pastime and delight.

HENRY WADSWORTH LONGFELLOW, *Outre-Mer*

Poetry, therefore, we will call *musical Thought*. The Poet is he who *thinks* in that manner.

THOMAS CARLYLE, *On Heroes and Hero-Worship*, 'The Hero as Poet'

I would define, in brief, the Poetry of words as the Rhythmical Creation of Beauty. Its sole arbiter is Taste.

EDGAR ALLAN POE, *The Poetic Principle*

Poetry is the spontaneous overflow of powerful feelings: it takes its origin from emotion recollected in tranquility.

WILLIAM WORDSWORTH, *Lyrical Ballads, Preface*

Poetry is like painting: one piece takes your fancy if you stand close to it, another if you keep at some distance.

HORACE, *Ars Poetica*

The essence of all poetry is to be found, not in high-wrought subtlety of thought, nor in pointed cleverness of phrase, but in the depths of the heart and the most sacred feelings of the men who write.

JOHN KEBLE, *Lectures on Poetry*

Poetry is truth in its Sunday clothes.

JOSEPH ROUX, *Meditations of a Parish Priest*

Poetry, native and true poetry, is nothing else than each poet's innermost feeling issuing in rhythmic language.

JOHN KEBLE, *Lectures on Poetry*

Poems very seldom consist of poetry and nothing else; and pleasure can be derived also from their other ingredients.

ALFRED EDWARD HOUSMAN, *The Name and Nature of Poetry*, Lecture delivered at Cambridge University, 9 May, 1933

Poetry implies the whole truth, philosophy expresses a part of it.

HENRY DAVID THOREAU, *Journal*, 26 June, 1852

Poetry is what Milton saw when he went blind.

DON MARQUIS, *The Sun Dial*

Not the poem which we have *read*, but that to which we *return*, with the greatest pleasure, possesses the genuine power, and claims the

name of *essential poetry*.
SAMUEL TAYLOR COLERIDGE, *Biographia Literaria*

Nobody, I think, ought to read poetry, or look at pictures or statues, who cannot find a great deal more in them than the poet or artist has actually expressed.
NATHANIEL HAWTHORNE, *The Marble Faun*

In every volume of poems something good may be found.
SAMUEL JOHNSON, Quoted in Boswell's *Life of Johnson*

A vein of poetry exists in the hearts of all men.
THOMAS CARLYLE, *On Heroes and Hero-Worship*,
'The Hero as Poet'

Doctors undertake a doctor's work; carpenters handle carpenter's tools: but, skilled or unskilled, we scribble poetry, all alike.
HORACE, *Epistles*

Poetry is an art, and chief of the fine arts: the easiest to dabble in, the hardest in which to reach true excellence.
EDMUND CLARENCE STEDMAN, *Victorian Poets*

If poetry comes not as naturally as leaves to a tree it had better not come at all.
JOHN KEATS, *Letter to John Taylor*, 1818

Great is the art of beginning, but greater the art is of ending;
Many a poem is marred by a superfluous verse.
HENRY WADSWORTH LONGFELLOW, *Elegiac Verse*

Poetry should surprise by a fine excess, and not by singularity; it should strike the reader as a wording of his own highest thoughts, and appear almost a remembrance.
JOHN KEATS, *Letter to John Taylor*, 1818

One merit of poetry few persons will deny: it says more and in fewer words than prose.

FRANÇOIS MARIE AROUET VOLTAIRE, *A Philosophical Dictionary*,
'Poets'

Poetry teaches the enormous force of a few words, and, in
proportion to the inspiration, checks loquacity.

RALPH WALDO EMERSON, *Parnassus*, Preface

When I struggle to be brief, I become obscure.

HORACE, *Ars Poetica*

Prose on certain occasions can bear a great deal of poetry: on the
other hand, poetry sinks and swoons under a moderate weight of
prose.

WALTER SAVAGE LANDOR, *Imaginary Conversations*,
'Archdeacon Hare and Walter Landor'

Poetry makes its own pertinence, and a single stanza outweighs a
book of prose.

RALPH WALDO EMERSON, *Journals*

Poetry is the record of the best and happiest moments of the
happiest and best minds.

PERCY BYSSHE SHELLEY, *A Defence of Poetry*

Science is for those who learn; poetry, for those who know.

JOSEPH ROUX, *Meditations of a Parish Priest*

A long poem is a test of invention which I take to be the Polar star of
poetry, as fancy is the sails, and imagination the rudder.

JOHN KEATS, *Letter to Benjamin Bailey*, 1817

Poetry is articulate painting, and painting is silent poetry.

PLUTARCH, *Moralia*, 'How to Study Poetry'

Poetry is certainly something more than good sense, but it must be
good sense at all events; just as a palace is more than a house, but it

must be a house, at least.

SAMUEL TAYLOR COLERIDGE, *Table Talk*

'Sir, what is poetry?'
'Why, Sir, it is much easier to say what it is not. We all *know* what light is; but it is not easy to *tell* what it is'.

LAURENCE STERNE, *Tristram Shandy*

The two cardinal points of poetry, the power of exciting the sympathy of the reader by a faithful adherence to the truth of nature, and the power of giving the interest of novelty by the modifying colours of imagination.

SAMUEL TAYLOR COLERIDGE, *Biographia Literaria*

A poem is made up of thoughts, each of which filled the whole sky of the poet in its turn.

RALPH WALDO EMERSON, *Journals*, 1834

Does he paint? he fain would write a poem –
Does he write? he fain would paint a picture.

ROBERT BROWNING, *One Word More*

There are pictures in poems and poems in pictures.

WILLIAM SCARBOROUGH, *Chinese Proverbs*

Poetry should be great and unobtrusive, a thing which enters into one's soul, and does not startle it or amaze it with itself, but with its subject.

JOHN KEATS, *Letter to J. H. Reynolds*, 1818

Prose is when all the lines except the last go on to the end. Poetry is when some of them fall short of it.

JEREMY BENTHAM, *Life of John Stuart Mill*

I always make the first verse well, but I have trouble making the others.

MOLIÈRE, *Les Précieuses Ridicules*

When my sonnet was rejected, I exclaimed, 'Damn the age; I will write for Antiquity!'

CHARLES LAMB, *Letter to B. W. Procter, 1829*

Poetry comes fine-spun from a mind at peace.

OVID, *Tristia*, Bk. I

*To have the deep Poetic heart*
*Is more than all poetic fame.*

ALFRED, LORD TENNYSON, *The New Timon*

Good sense is the body of poetic genius, fancy its drapery, motion its life, and imagination the soul.

SAMUEL TAYLOR COLERIDGE, *Biographia Literaria*

Poetry should be vital – either stirring our blood by its divine movements, or snatching our breath by its divine perfection. To do both is supreme glory, to do either is enduring fame.

AUGUSTINE BIRRELL, *Obiter Dicta*, 'Browning's Poetry'

Every good poem that I know I recalled by its rhythm also. Rhyme is a pretty good measure of the latitude and opulence of a writer. If unskilled, he is at once detected by the poverty of his chimes.

RALPH WALDO EMERSON, *Letters and Social Aims*,
'Poetry and Imagination'

There is no heroic poem in the world but is at bottom a biography, the life of a man; also it may be said, there is no life of a man, faithfully recorded, but is a heroic poem of its sort, rhymed or unrhymed.

THOMAS CARLYLE, *Essays*, 'Memoirs of Scott'

Poetry is the worst mask in the world behind which folly and stupidity could attempt to hide their features.

WILLIAM CULLEN BRYANT, *Lectures on Poetry*,
'The Nature of Poetry'

Poetry is a comforting piece of fiction set to more or less lascivious music.

HENRY LOUIS MENCKEN, *Prejudices*

When you write in prose you say what you mean. When you write in rhyme you say what you must.

OLIVER WENDELL HOLMES, *Over the Teacups*

Poetry has done enough when it charms, but prose must also convince.

HENRY LOUIS MENCKEN, *Prejudices*

Chinese poetry is of all poetry I know the most human and the least symbolic or romantic. It contemplates life just as it presents itself, without any veil of ideas, any rhetoric or sentiment; it simply clears away the obstruction which habit has built up between us and the beauty of things.

GOLDSWORTHY LOWES DICKINSON, *An Essay on the Civilizations of India, China, and Japan*

Poetry has been to me 'its own exceeding great reward'; it has soothed my afflictions; it has multiplied and refined my enjoyments; it has endeared solitude; and it has given me the habit of wishing to discover the good and the beautiful in all that meets and surrounds me.

SAMUEL TAYLOR COLERIDGE, *Biographia Literaria*

By labour and intent study (which I take to be my portion in this life) joined with the strong propensity of nature, I might perhaps leave something so written to after times, as they should not willingly let it die.

JOHN MILTON, *The Reason of Church Government*

As to my own Poems – they must be left to Providence and that fine sense of discrimination which I never cease to meditate upon and admire in the public: they cry out for new things and when you furnish them with what they cried for, 'it's *so* new', they grunt.

ROBERT BROWNING, *Letter to John Ruskin, 1855*

The crown of literature is poetry. . . . The writer of prose can only step aside when the poet passes.

SOMERSET MAUGHAM, *Saturday Review*, 1957

## Verses

Publishing a volume of verse is like dropping a rose-petal down the Grand Canyon and waiting for the echo.

DON MARQUIS, *The Sun Dial*

Even if nature says no, indignation makes me write verse.

JUVENAL, *Satires*

He's a Blockhead, that can't make two Verses; and he's a Fool that makes four.

THOMAS FULLER, *Gnomologia*

> *For rhyme the rudder is of verses,*
> *With which like ships they steer their courses.*
>
> SAMUEL BUTLER, *Hudibras*

> *But those that write in rhyme still make*
> *The one verse for the other's sake;*
> *For one for sense, and one for rhyme,*
> *I think's sufficient at one time.*
>
> SAMUEL BUTLER, *Ibid.*

> *Read Homer once, and you can read no more;*
> *For all books else appear so mean, so poor,*
> *Verse will seem prose; but still persist to read,*
> *And Homer will be all the books you need.*
>
> JOHN SHEFFIELD, DUKE OF BUCKINGHAM AND NORMANBY,
> *Essay on Poetry*

Anyone may be an honourable man, and yet write verse badly.

MOLIÈRE, *Le Misanthrope*

No one will ever get at my verses who insists upon viewing them as a literary performance.

WALT WHITMAN, *A Backward Glance O'er Travel'd Roads*

All good verses are like impromptus made at leisure.

JOSEPH JOUBERT, *Pensées*

> *How many verses have I thrown*
> *Into the fire because the one*
> *Peculiar word, the wanted most,*
> *Was irrecoverably lost.*
>
> WALTER SAVAGE LANDOR, *Verses – Why Burnt*

Barefaced poverty drove me to writing verses.

HORACE, *Epistles*

# 9
# One's Own Library

No furniture so charming as books.

SYDNEY SMITH, *Lady Holland, Memoir*

There is no mood to which a man may not administer the appropriate medicine at the cost of reaching down a volume from his bookshelf.

ARTHUR JAMES BALFOUR, *Essays and Addresses*

Consider what you have in the smallest chosen library. A company of the wisest and wittiest men that could be picked out of all civil countries, in a thousand years, have set in best order the results of their learning and wisdom. The men themselves were hid and inaccessible, solitary, impatient of interruption, fenced by etiquette; but the thought which they did not uncover to their bosom friend is here written out in transparent words to us, the strangers of another age.

RALPH WALDO EMERSON, *Society and Solitude, 'Books'*

Affect not as some do that bookish ambition to be stored with books and have well-furnished libraries, yet keep their heads empty of knowledge; to desire to have many books, and never to use them, is like a child that will have a candle burning by him all the while he is sleeping.

HENRY PEACHAM, *The Compleat Gentleman*

Th' first thing to have in a libry is a shelf. Fr'm time to time this can be decorated with lithrachure. But th' shelf is th' main thing.

FINLEY PETER DUNNE, *Books, Mr Dooley Says*

Good as it is to inherit a library, it is better to collect one.
AUGUSTINE BIRRELL, *Obiter Dicta*, 'Book-Buying'

A great library contains the diary of the human race.
REV. GEORGE DAWSON, Address on opening of the
Birmingham Free Library, 1866

Every library should try to be complete on something, if it were only the history of pin-heads.
OLIVER WENDELL HOLMES, *The Poet at the Breakfast Table*

I do not understand; I pause; I examine.
MICHEL DE MONTAIGNE, *Inscription for his Library*

A quotation, a chance word heard in an unexpected quarter, puts me on the trail of the book destined to achieve some intellectual advancement in me.
GEORGE MOORE, *Confessions of a Young Man*

I go into my library, and all history rolls before me. I breathe the morning air of the world while the scent of Eden's roses yet lingered in it . . . I see the pyramids building; I hear the shoutings of the armies of Alexander . . . I sit as in a theatre – the stage is time, the play is the play of the world.
ALEXANDER SMITH, *Dreamthorp*, 'Books and Gardens'

Books are a world in themselves, it is true; but they are not the only world. The world itself is a volume larger than all the libraries in it.
WILLIAM HAZLITT, *On the Conversation of Authors*,
'The Plain Speaker'

Great collections of books are subject to certain accidents besides the damp, the worms, and the rats; one not less common is that of the *borrowers*, not to say a word of the purloiners.
ISAAC D'ISRAELI, *Curiosities of Literature*,
'The Bibliomania'

I mean your *borrower of books* – those mutilators of collections,

spoilers of the symmetry of shelves, and creators of odd volumes.
CHARLES LAMB, *The Two Races of Men*

> *Knowing I loved my books, he furnish'd me*
> *From mine own library with volumes that*
> *I prize above my dukedom.*
> WILLIAM SHAKESPEARE, *The Tempest*

He that revels in a well-chosen library, has innumerable dishes, and all of admirable flavour.
WILLIAM GODWIN, *The Enquirer*, 'Early Taste for Reading'

> *Come, and take choice of all my library,*
> *And so beguile thy sorrow.*
> WILLIAM SHAKESPEARE, *Titus Andronicus*

A Man's library is a sort of harem, and tender readers have a great pudency in showing their books to a stranger.
RALPH WALDO EMERSON, *Society and Solitude*, 'Books'

Novels are sweets. All people with healthy literary appetites love them – almost all women; a vast number of clever, hard-headed men.
WILLIAM MAKEPEACE THACKERAY, *The Roundabout Papers*,
'On a Lazy, Idle Boy'

For the most part, our novel-reading is a passion for results.
RALPH WALDO EMERSON, *In Praise of Books*,
'The Conduct of Life'

What a place to be in is an old library! It seems as though all the souls of all the writers, that have bequeathed their labours to these Bodleians, were reposing here, as in some dormitory, or middle state. I do not want to handle, to profane the leaves, their winding-sheets. I could as soon dislodge a shade. I seem to inhale learning, walking amid their foliage; and the odour of their old moth-scented coverings is fragrant as the first bloom of those sciential apples which grew amid the happy orchard.

        CHARLES LAMB, *Essays of Elia*, 'Oxford in the Vacation'

A circulating library in a town is as an ever-green tree of diabolical knowledge! It blossoms through the year.

        RICHARD BRINSLEY SHERIDAN, *The Rivals*

No place affords a more striking conviction of the vanity of human hopes, than a public library.

        SAMUEL JOHNSON, *The Rambler*, 1751

# 10
# Critics

Ah! don't say you agree with me. When people agree with me I
always feel that I must be wrong.

OSCAR WILDE, *The Critic as Artist*

> *Let us teach others who themselves excel*
> *And censure freely who have written well,*
> *Authors are partial to their wit 'tis true;*
> *But are not critics to their judgment too?*
> ALEXANDER POPE, *An Essay on Criticism*

If an author write better than his contemporaries, they will term him
a plagiarist; if as well, a pretender; but if worse, he may stand some
chance of commendation as a genius of some promise, from whom
much may be expected by a due attention to their good counsel and
advice.

CHARLES CALEB COLTON, *Lacon*

> *A perfect judge will read each work of wit*
> *With the same spirit that its author writ.*
> ALEXANDER POPE, *An Essay on Criticism*

The opinion of a great body of the reading public is very materially
influenced by the unsupported assertions of those who assume a
right to criticise.

LORD MACAULAY, *Essays*, 'Montgomery's Poems'

> *You puff the poets of other days,*
> *The living you deplore.*

> *Spare me the accolade: your praise*
> *Is not worth dying for.*
>
> MARTIAL, *Epigrams*

I would rather be attacked than unnoticed. For the worst thing you can do to an author is to be silent as to his works.

SAMUEL JOHNSON, Quoted in *Boswell's Life of Johnson*

Pay no attention to what the critics say; no statue has ever been put up to a critic.

JEAN SIBELIUS, *Attributed*

The critic should describe, and not prescribe.

EUGÈNE IONESCO, *Improvisation*

You can spot the bad critic when he starts by discussing the poet and not the poem.

EZRA POUND, *A, B, C of Reading*

A good critic is the man who describes his adventures among masterpieces.

ANATOLE FRANCE, *La Vie Littéraire*, Preface

There is no reward so delightful, no pleasure so exquisite, as having one's work known and acclaimed by those whose applause confers honour.

MOLIÈRE, *The Would-be Gentleman*

> *A man must serve his time to every trade*
> *Save censure – critics are all ready made.*
> LORD BYRON, *English Bards and Scotch Reviewers*

A true critic ought to dwell rather upon excellencies than imperfections, to discover the concealed beauties of a writer, and communicate to the world such things as are worth their observation.

JOSEPH ADDISON, *The Spectator*, No. 291

When a man says he sees nothing in a book, he very often means that

he does not see himself in it: which, if it is not a comedy or a satire, is
likely enough.

JULIUS CHARLES HARE and AUGUSTUS WILLIAM HARE,
*Guesses at Truth*

He's the kind of man that gets up a reputation for being clever and
artistic by running down the very one particular thing that every one
likes, and cracking up some book or picture or play that no one has
ever heard of.

FRANK NORRIS, *The Pit*

To be occasionally quoted is the only fame I care for.
ALEXANDER SMITH, *Dreamthorp*, 'Men of Letters'

Classical quotation is the *parole* of literary men all over the world.
SAMUEL JOHNSON, Quoted in Boswell's *Life of Johnson*

> Some judge of authors' names, not works, and then
> Nor praise nor blame the writings, but the men.
> ALEXANDER POPE, *Essay on Criticism*

There is no luck in literary reputation. They who make up the final
verdict upon every book are not the partial and noisy readers of the
hour when it appears; but a court as of angels, a public not to be
bribed, not to be entreated, and not to be overawed, decides upon
every man's title to fame.

RALPH WALDO EMERSON, *Essays*, First Series, 'Spiritual Laws'

If the men of wit and genius would resolve never to complain in their
works of critics and detractors, the next age would not know that
they ever had any.

JONATHAN SWIFT, *Thoughts on Various Subjects*

The critic in *The Vicar of Wakefield* lays down that you should
*always* say that the picture would have been better if the painter had
taken more pains; but in the case of the practised literary man, you
should often enough say that the writings would have been much

better if the writer had taken less pains.

WALTER BAGEHOT, *Literary Studies*, 'Shakespeare'

It is only about things that do not interest one that one can give a really unbiased opinion, which is no doubt the reason why an unbiased opinion is always absolutely valueless.

OSCAR WILDE, *The Critic as Artist*

No publisher should ever express an opinion of the value of what he publishes. That is a matter entirely for the literary critic to decide.

OSCAR WILDE, *Letter in St James's Gazette*,
28 June, 1890

You do not publish your own verses, Laelius; you criticise mine. Pray cease to criticise mine, or else publish your own.

MARTIAL, *Epigrams*

For God's sake (I never was more serious) don't make me ridiculous any more by terming me *gentle-hearted* in print . . . substitute drunken dog, ragged head, seld-shaver, odd-eyed, stuttering, or any other epithet which truly and properly belongs to the gentleman in question.

CHARLES LAMB, *Letter to Coleridge*, August, 1800

You know who critics are? – the men who have failed in literature and art.

BENJAMIN DISRAELI, *Lothair*

Taking to pieces is the trade of those who cannot construct.

RALPH WALDO EMERSON, *Journals*, 1858

He who would write and can't write, can surely review.

JAMES RUSSELL LOWELL, *A Fable for Critics*

Reviewers are usually people who would have been poets, historians, biographers, if they could; they have tried their talents at one or the other, and have failed; therefore they turn critics.

SAMUEL TAYLOR COLERIDGE, *Lectures, Shakespeare and Milton*

Reviewers are forever telling authors they can't understand them.
The author might often reply: Is that my fault?

JULIUS CHARLES HARE and AUGUSTUS WILLIAM HARE,
*Guesses at Truth*

*They who write ill, and they who ne'er durst write,*
*Turn critics out of mere revenge and spite.*

JOHN DRYDEN, *Conquest of Granada*, Prologue

What a blessed thing it is that Nature, when she invented,
manufactured and patented her authors, contrived to make critics
out of the chips that were left!

OLIVER WENDELL HOLMES, *The Professor at the Breakfast Table*

If certain Critics were as clear-sighted as they are malignant, how
great would be the benefit to be derived from their writings.

PERCY BYSSHE SHELLEY, *The Revolt of Islam*, Preface

Critics are sentinels in the grand army of letters, stationed at the
corners of newspapers and reviews, to challenge every new author.

HENRY WADSWORTH LONGFELLOW, *Kavanagh*

A critic is a man who expects miracles.

JAMES HUNEKER, *Iconoclasts*

The aim of criticism is to distinguish what is essential in the work of
a writer. It is the delight of a critic to praise; but praise is scarcely
part of his duty . . . What we ask of him is that he should find out for
us more than we can find out for ourselves.

ARTHUR SYMONS, Introduction to Coleridge's
*Biographia Literaria*

*Some have at first for wits, then poets pass'd,*
*Turn'd critics next, and prov'd plain fools at last.*

ALEXANDER POPE, *An Essay on Criticism*

It may be well said that these wretched men know not what they do.
They scatter their insults and their slanders without heed as to

whether the poisoned shaft lights on a heart made callous by many
blows, or one, like Keats', composed of more penetrable stuff.

PERCY BYSSHE SHELLEY, *Adonais*, Preface

*Whoever thinks a faultless piece to see,*
*Thinks that ne'er was, nor is, no 'er shall be.*
*In every work regard the writer' end,*
*Since none can compass more than they intend.*
*And if the means be just, the conduct true,*
*Applause, in spite of trivial faults, is due.*

ALEXANDER POPE, *Essay on Criticism*

The skin of a man of letters is peculiarly sensitive to the bite of the
critical mosquito; and he lives in a climate in which such mosquitoes
swarm. He is seldom stabbed to the heart – he is often killed by pin-
pricks.

ALEXANDER SMITH, *Dreamthorp*, 'Men of Letters'

*He could gauge the old books by the old set of rules,*
*And his very old nothings pleased very old fools;*
*But give him a new book, fresh out of the heart,*
*And you put him at sea without compass or chart.*

JAMES RUSSEL LOWELL, *A Fable for Critics*

There is nothing which we receive with so much reluctance as
advice.

JOSEPH ADDISON, *The Spectator*, No. *512*

It is through criticism . . . that the race has managed to come out of
the woods and lead a civilized life. The first man who objected to the
general nakedness, and advised his fellows to put on clothes, was the
first critic.

EDWIN LAWRENCE GODKIN, *Problems of Modern Democracy*

A drama critic is a man who leaves no turn unstoned.

GEORGE BERNARD SHAW, *The New York Times*, 1950

. . . the play was a great success. But the audience was a failure.

OSCAR WILDE, When asked to comment on the reception
of one of his least successful plays

Speak of the moderns without contempt and the ancients without idolatry; judge them all by their merits, but not by their age.

LORD CHESTERFIELD, *Letter to his son*, 1748

What the mulberry leaf is to the silkworm, the author's book, treatise, essay, poem, is to the critical larvae that feed upon it. It furnishes them with food and clothing.

OLIVER WENDELL HOLMES, *Over the Teacups*

He who first praises a book becomingly is next in merit to the author.

WALTER SAVAGE LANDOR, *Imaginary Conversations*,
Alfieri and Salomon

## Criticism

Criticism should not be querulous and wasting, all knife and root-puller, but guiding, instructive, inspiring, a south wind, not an east wind.

RALPH WALDO EMERSON, *Journals*

Of all the cants which are canted in this canting world, though the cant of hypocrites may be the worst, the cant of criticism is the most tormenting.

LAURENCE STERNE, *Tristram Shandy*

I am never indifferent, and never pretend to be, to what people say or think of my books. They are my children, and I like to have them liked.

HENRY WADSWORTH LONGFELLOW,
*Letter to Richard Henry Stoddard*, 1878

Get your enemies to read your works in order to mend them, for your friend is so much your second self that he will judge too like you.

ALEXANDER POPE, *An Essay on Criticism*

It is a good lesson – though it may often be a hard one – for a man who has dreamed of literary fame . . . to step aside out of the narrow circle in which his claims are recognized, and to find how utterly devoid of significance, beyond that circle, is all that he achieves, and all he aims at.

NATHANIEL HAWTHORNE, *The Scarlet Letter*,
'The Custom House'

They have a right to censure that have a heart to help.

WILLIAM PENN, *Some Fruits of Solitude*

I am bound by my own definition of criticism: a disinterested endeavour to learn and propagate the best that is known and thought in the world.

MATTHEW ARNOLD, *Essays in Criticism*,
'Functions of Criticism at the Present Time'

When I read the rules of criticism, I immediately inquire after the works of the author who has written them, and by that means discover what it is he likes in a composition.

JOSEPH ADDISON, *The Guardian, No. 115*

Criticism comes easier than craftsmanship.

ZEUXIS, Quoted in Pliny's *Natural History*

Opinion is ultimately determined by the feelings, and not by the intellect.

HERBERT SPENCER, *Social Statics*

Criticism is like champagne: nothing more execrable if bad, nothing more excellent if good.

CHARLES CALEB COLTON, *Lacon*

One of the commonest but most uncritical faults of criticism – the refusal to consider what it is that the author intended to give us.

GEORGE SAINTSBURY, *Preface to Fielding's Tom Jones*

I find the pain of a little censure, even when it is unfounded, is more acute than the pleasure of much praise.

THOMAS JEFFERSON, *Writings*

Works of art are of an infinite loneliness and with nothing so little to be reached as with criticism.

RAINER MARIA RILKE, *Letters to a Young Poet*, 1903

A great deal of contemporary criticism reads to me like a man saying: 'Of course I do not like green cheese: I am very fond of brown sherry.'

G. K. CHESTERTON, *All I Survey*, '*On Jonathan Swift*'

We find fault with perfection itself.

BLAISE PASCAL, *Pensées*

We can never know that a piece of writing is bad unless we have begun by trying to read it as if it was very good and ended by discovering that we were paying the author an undeserved compliment.

C. S. LEWIS, *Experiment in Criticism*

> *Some praise at morning what they blame at night,*
> *But always think the last opinion right.*

ALEXANDER POPE, *An Essay on Criticism*

People ask you for criticism, but they only want praise.

SOMERSET MAUGHAM, *Of Human Bondage*

Advice is seldom welcome; and those who want it the most always like it the least.

LORD CHESTERFIELD, *Letter to his son*, 1748

What a sense of security in an old book which Time has criticized for us!

JAMES RUSSELL LOWELL, *Literary Essays*,
Library of old Authors

# Index of Authors

*Authors with more than one quotation on the page are marked with an asterisk \* (e.g. Thomas Carlyle 2\*).*